D0791407

101 KIDS ACTIVITIES

THAT ARE THE OOEY, GOOEY-EST EVER!

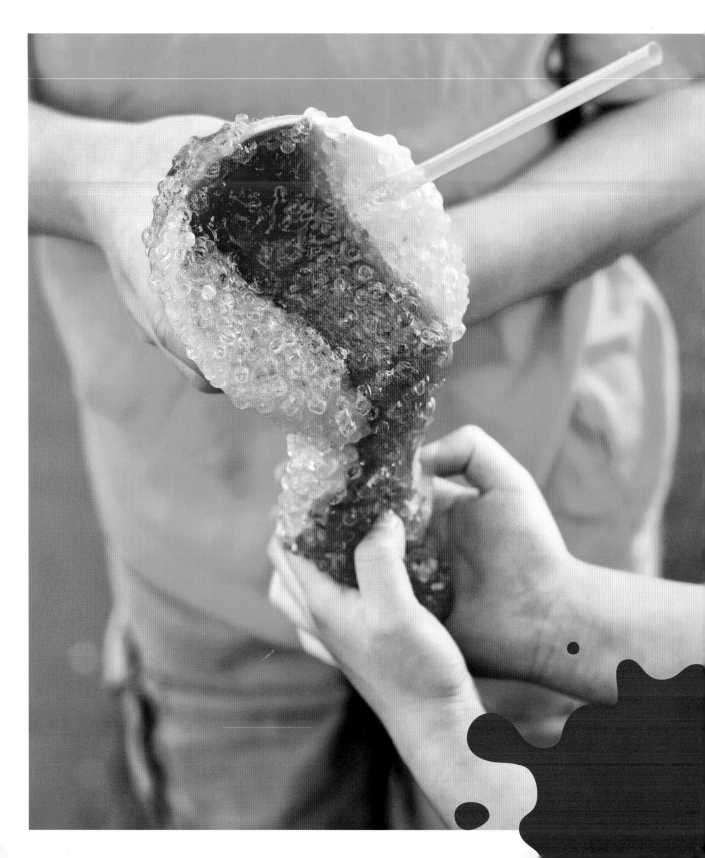

Harrington, Jamie,
101 Kids activities
that are the ooey, gooey
2018.
33305244372342
ca   04/03/19

101 KIDS ACTIVITIES

THAT ARE THE OOEY, GOOEY-EST EVER!

NONSTOP FUN WITH DIY
SLIMES, DOUGHS AND MOLDABLES

JAMIE HARRINGTON, BRITTANIE PYPER AND HOLLY HOMER

BESTSELLING AUTHORS OF *101 KIDS ACTIVITIES,*
THE 101 COOLEST SIMPLE SCIENCE EXPERIMENTS
AND ADORKABLE BUBBLE BATH CRAFTS

PAGE STREET
PUBLISHING CO.

PAGE STREET
PUBLISHING CO.

Copyright © 2018 Jamie Harrington, Brittanie Pyper and Holly Homer

First published in 2018 by
Page Street Publishing Co
27 Congress Street, Suite 105
Salem, MA 01970

www.pagestreetpublishing.com

All rights reserved. No part of this book may be reproduced or used, in any form or by any
means, electronic or mechanical, without prior permission in writing from the publisher.

Distributed by Macmillan, sales in Canada by The Canadian Manda Group.

22 21 20 19 18   1 2 3 4 5

ISBN-13: 978-1-62414-661-9
ISBN-10: 1-62414-661-9

Library of Congress Control Number: 2018938285

Cover and book design by Meg Baskis for Page Street Publishing Co.
Photography by Holly Homer, Jamie Harrington and Brittanie Pyper

Printed and bound in China

Page Street Publishing protects our planet by donating to nonprofits like
The Trustees, which focuses on local land conservation.

FOR HALLE, KAYZEN, TAREK, RYAN, REID AND RHETT, BECAUSE YOU'RE THE REASON WE STILL ACT LIKE KIDS EVERY DAY.

CONTENTS

INTRODUCTION

Ooey, gooey, sparkly, slimy, smelly, colorful. When you think about superfun, creative play, what words come to your mind? Play is when you get to let your creativity and your imagination soar. You can be or do whatever suits you. You can become a mad scientist, a Jurassic dinosaur, a doctor, a mud monster or even a sparkly fairy. The sky is the limit! If you can awaken your imagination in the depths of your mind, you can be or do anything.

One of the best ways to play is with slimes, doughs and things you can mold. It's easy to have fun when you're getting all wet and sticky! These recipes and concoctions will give you something awesome to do for hours on end. Oh, and they're fun for moms and dads, too, because everyone loves to squeeze something squishy!

Playtime is more than just fun and games. It helps teach you, by growing and developing your imagination and guiding you through steps to help you reach a bigger goal. Yeah, you will have great fun, but it's so much more!

This book is full of exciting, fantastical, even scientific recipes that help you create, learn and bring out that spirit of play. Whether it's a slime, a dough or some other moldable creation, you will be able to create and become your imagination's greatest work of artistry.

Holly Homer   Jamie Harrington   Brittanie Pyper

SLIME

It wiggles, it jiggles and it slithers in your hands.
It's the perfect combination of fun and science.
The crazy thing about slime is that when you start,
everything is separated, but then the ingredients
come together and activate each other to form
something you've never felt before.

Slime can be gooey and gross, like frog's vomit
(page 20) or a sack of spiders (page 32). Or it can be
supersilly, like a melted snowman (page 19) or cronch
(page 37). You never know what you're going
to slime together!

MAGNETIC SLIME

ADULT SUPERVISION

DO NOT EAT

Magnetic slime might just be the most awesome thing you've ever played with! It is a slimy, black goo that seems to eat and crawl toward magnets! Can you really make this right in your own home? Yes!

INGREDIENTS

1 (4-oz [118-ml]) bottle white school glue

¼ cup (60 ml) water

¼ cup (60 ml) liquid starch

2 to 4 tsp (8 to 16 g) black iron oxide powder (you can find this online)

EQUIPMENT

Bowl

Spoon

Neodymium magnet (a cylindrical magnet that is magnetized on the ends)

WHAT YOU DO

Add the school glue to a bowl and stir in the water using the spoon. Once it's fully mixed, add the liquid starch and stir until it starts to come together like slime. Remove the slippery goo from the bowl and knead it with your hands, stretching it to make it more slime-ish. At this point, you have a bunch of white goo.

Now it's time to add the iron oxide powder. This is what makes the slime magically magnetic! Use your thumbs to make a small indentation in the slime. With an adult's help, add a teaspoon (4 g) of iron oxide powder to the dent in your slime. Fold the slime over the powder and knead it with your hands to make the powder mix into the goop. The slime will turn black. Repeat until you've added enough powder to the slime to make it react to the neodymium magnet. The slime should pull up toward the magnet when it is held above the slime. It will also appear to "eat" the magnet when it is placed in the center of the slime. So cool! You will want to play with this "magic" slime for hours!

TIPS

☐ **Store in an airtight container.**

◇ **Refresh with water.**

ECTOPLASM

DO NOT EAT

Otherwise known as ghost slime, this boogery substance is as easy to make as its name is fun to say! With ooey, gooey goodness that's equally gross in the light or the dark, you can pretend to hunt ghosts like a professional.

INGREDIENTS

1 (16-oz [454-g]) box cornstarch

1½ cups (360 ml) water

15 drops neon green food coloring

2 tbsp (30 ml) green glow-in-the-dark paint (optional)

EQUIPMENT

Bowl

WHAT YOU DO

In a bowl, mix the cornstarch and water into a goo with your hands. Add the food coloring until your desired color is reached. This really could not be easier!

To make it glow-in-the-dark, squish in about 2 tablespoons (30 ml) of green glow-in-the-dark paint for a cool effect. Make sure you hold the concoction up to a bright light for about 2 minutes to activate it.

TIPS

☐ **Store in an airtight container.**

◇ **Refresh with water.**

PUDDING SLIME

ADULT SUPERVISION   EDIBLE

Pudding Slime? Can you taste it? Yes, you can! Gross out your friends by tasting this crazy creation in front of them, then tell them your secret ingredient. You are sure to get giggles and have your friends begging to play with Pudding Slime too.

INGREDIENTS

2 (3.4-oz [96-g]) packets of instant pudding in your favorite flavor

1 packet of matching flavor powdered drink mix

1 cup (160 g) cornstarch, divided

½ cup (120 ml) hot water

EQUIPMENT

Bowl

Spoon

WHAT YOU DO

Add the pudding, drink mix and ½ cup (80 g) of the cornstarch to a bowl. Start mixing. Ask an adult to help you stir in the hot water slowly, mixing the whole time. Be careful! Remember the water is hot! Add the remaining cornstarch slowly. Stir it all together. It will be very sticky at first, but like with any slime, the more you work with it, the better it will get. If it is too wet, add a teaspoon at a time of cornstarch. If it is too dry, add a teaspoon at a time of warm water.

Want to experiment? Add different flavors of drink mix to see what colors you end up with!

☐ **Store in an airtight container.**

◊ **Refresh with water.**

POMEGRANATE SLIME

ADULT SUPERVISION

DO NOT EAT

Have you ever tasted a pomegranate? With an adult's permission, taste some of the seeds before you add them to this gooey mixture. You will get a tangy, sweet and sour taste. Not only are the seeds yummy, they add bumpy fun to your goopy slime concoction.

INGREDIENTS

1 large pomegranate

1 cup (240 ml) water

1 (5-oz [147-ml]) bottle clear liquid school glue

¾ cup (180 ml) liquid starch (you can find this in the laundry aisle)

EQUIPMENT

Large bowl

Spoon (optional)

WHAT YOU DO

Have an adult cut open the pomegranate. Pick out as many seeds as you can. Put the seeds in your bowl. Be very careful! Even small amounts of pomegranate juice can stain! Add the water, glue and liquid starch to the bowl. Smoosh and goosh it all up with your hands (or a spoon if you prefer) until it's a red glob of textured, slimy goo.

TIPS

Have a roll of paper towels on hand. This can get messy, and can stain.

Want to try a fun way to get the seeds out of the fruit? If you have an adult cut the pomegranate in half, you can hit the skin of the fruit with your spoon while holding it over the bowl. The seeds should fall out into the bowl.

☐ Store in an airtight container.

🕐 Limited shelf life.

💧 Refresh with water.

SLUDGE MONSTER

ADULT SUPERVISION

DO NOT EAT

Have you seen a sludge monster? A sludge monster is a slimy glob of goo who isn't very smart. We don't know what his feet look like, or if he even has feet, because he is always covered in gloop. He lives in the sewers of the city, and eats the dirtiest of dirty garbage. Make your own gooey Sludge Monster, and let your imagination fly.

INGREDIENTS

1½ cups (360 ml) warm water, divided

1 (4-oz [118-ml]) bottle white school glue

1 tsp of food coloring in your favorite monster color

1 tsp borax

2 figurines that will be used just for the Sludge Monster slime

EQUIPMENT

2 bowls

Spoon

WHAT YOU DO

In one bowl, mix ½ cup (120 ml) of warm water with the bottle of glue and food coloring. Mix this up well with a spoon.

In the second bowl, using the spoon, mix 1 cup (240 ml) of warm water with the borax until dissolved. Pour the bowl of borax water into the bowl of colorful glue water. Count out loud to twenty and watch the gooey science magic happen! Then stir the mix with the spoon. Use your hands to hold the goo back, then pour out the extra water so you have just the goo. It will be very sticky. Knead it, pound it with your fist, squish it and push it. Pour out the extra water one more time. Play with the goo until it is no longer sticky. Now grab those figurines! Cover them in the goo, and you have instant sludge monsters.

TIPS

☐ **Store in an airtight container.**

◯ **Refresh with water.**

MELTED-SNOWMAN SLIME

ADULT SUPERVISION

DO NOT EAT

You loved your snowman when you made him on that ice-cold day, but then he was gone. Not now! This creation lets you keep your snowman all year long! Although he may be a little melted, he will always be your snowman friend. (And maybe "he" will be a "she!")

INGREDIENTS

½ cup (120 ml) water

½ cup (120 ml) washable white glue

½ cup (120 ml) liquid starch

EQUIPMENT

Bowl

Spoon or craft stick

Snowman parts (googly eyes, buttons and colored foam sheets cut into a scarf, a hat and a nose)

WHAT YOU DO

Mix the water and glue in a bowl. Use a spoon or craft stick and mix it well. Pour in the liquid starch. Watch closely as the slime forms right before your eyes. It will be pretty sticky at first, but mix that goo up with your hands. You will feel it become less watery and more slimy. This is what you want. The more you play with it, the more like real slime it becomes. After about 15 minutes of playing with it, kneading it, punching it and rolling it, you will have a perfect melted-snowman consistency. If you have excess liquid after the slime forms, just discard it.

You can do two things with the slime. You can make the snowman stand up and quickly add the snowman parts, then watch him melt away before your eyes. Or you can flatten out the goo and place the snowman parts on top. It will look like you have a perfectly melted snowman.

TIPS

☐ **Store in an airtight container.**

◌ **Refresh with water.**

FROG'S VOMIT SLIME

ADULT SUPERVISION

DO NOT EAT

Here's the deal: there's nothing ooier or gooier than frog's vomit. Frog's Vomit Slime is crazy stretchy, and it's even got a little gross surprise inside! Don't be scared though, no actual frogs are involved.

INGREDIENTS

1 cup (240 ml) clear school glue

2 cups (480 ml) warm water, divided

2 drops green food coloring

3 drops yellow food coloring

Lime essential oil (optional)

1 tsp borax powder (you can find this in the laundry aisle)

Mini-fly toys

EQUIPMENT

Large bowl

Spoon or craft stick

Plastic cup

WHAT YOU DO

Measure out the clear glue into the large bowl. Add 1 cup (240 ml) of warm water, the food coloring and the optional lime essential oil. Stir the mixture until it all comes together.

Mix the remaining 1 cup (240 ml) of warm water and the borax powder together in the plastic cup. Slowly pour the contents of the plastic cup into the glue mixture and stir until the slime starts to form. You might end up kneading the slime with your hands for a few minutes to get it to form. Sprinkle your mini-flies into the Frog's Vomit and get them squished all in the slime. Now it's time to play!

TIPS

☐ Store in an airtight container.

⬭ Refresh with water.

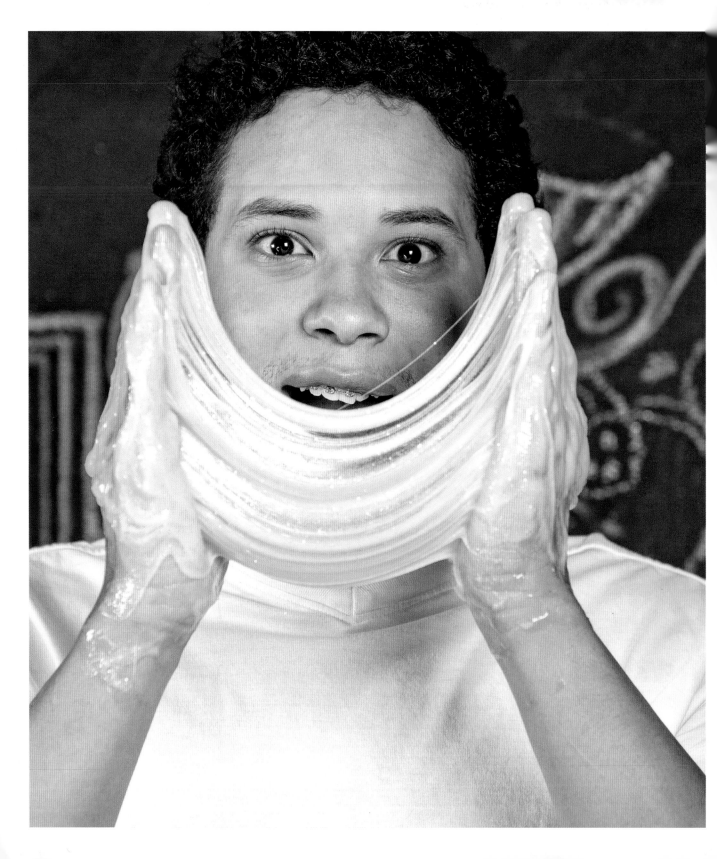

UNICORN SNOT

ADULT SUPERVISION

DO NOT EAT

Why? Because, unicorns are magical. Everything about them just screams . . . CUTE! Even their glittery boogers are sparkly and fun.

INGREDIENTS

1 (5-oz [147-ml]) bottle clear school glue

2 tbsp (30 ml) water

A few drops of food coloring (What colors would a unicorn sneeze?)

2 tbsp (48 g) glitter (silver, pink or purple works great)

½ cup (120 ml) liquid starch

EQUIPMENT

Large bowl

Spoon

2 or 3 small clear jars with lids (optional)

WHAT YOU DO

First of all, cover your work surface. Glitter is one of those things that likes to multiply and get in areas you didn't know existed.

Now, dump your glue, water, food coloring and glitter into a bowl. Stir that up well with the spoon. Add your liquid starch. You will see it start to form the slime. Squeeze, squish and squash the slime all over the bowl. You will have water and starch drip away from the slime and into the bowl. This is okay! You are making your snot! Now, take the slime and knead it for about 15 minutes to get the right texture.

TIPS

If 2 tablespoons (48 g) of glitter isn't enough for you, go wild! Add another tablespoon (24 g).

Store in a clear jar as a room decoration!

☐ Store in an airtight container.

⬡ Refresh with water.

ADULT
SUPERVISION

DO NOT
EAT

I SPY SLIME

You know those cool *iSpy* books? This slime is like that, but in gooey, slithery form! You can play with this slime with your friends and make it a game! See who can find the most items the fastest.

INGREDIENTS

1 batch of Clear Slime (page 74)

½ cup (120 g) of spangle mix and beads

EQUIPMENT

Large bowl

Spoon

WHAT YOU DO

Once the clear slime is made, it's time to add your mix-ins. Squish your spangle mix and beads into your slime. Now pick up the slime and squish it in your hands. Are you able to spy all your trinkets?

TIPS

☐ **Store in an airtight container.**

◊ **Refresh with water.**

PILLOW SLIME

ADULT SUPERVISION

DO NOT EAT

Want a slime that is as soft and fluffy as a pillow? This slime is sure to do the trick. It's from our friend Avery Ivanovsky of BoJo Slime. Just beware: it is so soft, it might even put you to sleep!

INGREDIENTS

2 tsp (6 g) instant snow

1 cup plus 2 tbsp (270 ml) water, divided

1 cup (240 ml) clear school glue

Food coloring (optional)

Essential oils for smell (optional)

1 tsp borax

EQUIPMENT

2 bowls

Spoon

Food storage container

WHAT YOU DO

First add the instant snow into one bowl and then add enough water to make it resemble slush (about 2 tablespoons [30 ml]). Next, pour the glue into your slushy mixture. Add in your optional color and scent, if you like.

In a separate bowl, mix 1 cup (240 ml) of warm water and borax until the borax is dissolved. Slowly pour the borax solution into the glue mixture until the slime is thick enough to stretch slightly, but not sticky. Set it in a clear airtight container for at least 3 days. This allows your Pillow Slime to clear up and sets the texture. Once it's ready, play and have fun!

TIPS

☐ **Store in an airtight container.**

💧 **Refresh with water.**

AVALANCHE SLIME

ADULT SUPERVISION

DO NOT EAT

This is the coolest thing ever. The two slimes together look like ice and snow. The colors seem to fall and slide, creating your own avalanche. Take it out to play, and you will have a marble-looking goo. Don't be scared by the long directions. It's really easy to make!

INGREDIENTS

½ cup plus 1¼ tsp (126 ml) saline solution (make sure it says buffered on the package), divided

1 tsp baking soda, divided

1 (5-oz [147-ml]) bottle clear school glue

1 (4-oz [118-ml]) bottle white school glue

2 colors of gel food coloring

EQUIPMENT

1 jar or drinking glass

Spoon

Bowl

Clear 1-cup (240-ml) food storage container

Popsicle stick

TIP ☐ **Store in an airtight container.**

WHAT YOU DO

Squeeze the saline solution into the jar or glass. Add ½ teaspoon of the baking soda. Stir until it is dissolved. Dump your whole bottle of clear glue into the solution. Do not stir! Let it sit. Go to the next step.

Pour your bottle of white glue into the bowl. Add ½ teaspoon of baking soda and stir it up using the spoon. Now, squirt about 1 teaspoon of the saline solution into the white-glue mixture (just eyeball it). Start to stir. Add about ¼ teaspoon of the saline solution until the slime starts to form. The more saline solution you add, the stiffer it will become. It is ready when it starts to pull away from the sides of the bowl.

Take the white slime out of the bowl. Stretch and play with this goop in your hands until it's not sticky anymore.

Now, go back to the clear mixture. Slowly stir it up with a spoon until a stiff slime forms. Take the clear slime out of the jar or glass. Squeeze it a bit to get the extra solution out, then place it in the bottom of the food storage container. Using the popsicle stick, "paint" one color of food coloring on half of the clear slime. Use the other color for the other half of the slime, painting it on with the popsicle stick. Place the white slime on top of your colorful masterpiece, filling up the rest of the food container. Put the lid tightly on the container, and turn the container upside down. Let it sit for about 24 hours. When the time is up, look at your beautiful creation! It will look like the color slid into the white slime! You can now take it out and play with it. It will create a beautiful marbled color as you play with it.

FISHBOWL SLIME

ADULT SUPERVISION   DO NOT EAT

Spending time at the ocean is fun. Don't you just wish you could scoop some of it up and take it with you when the vacation is over? Now you can make your very own slime that looks just like the ocean. It is an instant mini-vacation!

INGREDIENTS

1 large (9-oz [266-ml]) bottle clear school glue

½ tsp baking soda

10 to 15 drops blue food coloring

¼ cup (60 ml) clear acrylic vase filler (you can get this at any craft store)

About 2 tbsp (30 ml) saline solution (make sure it says buffered on the package)

Small plastic sea creatures (optional)

EQUIPMENT

Small clear fishbowl or large bowl

Spoon

WHAT YOU DO

Empty the bottle of glue into the fish bowl. Stir in the baking soda, food coloring and vase filler. Mix it all up with the spoon. Add about 1 teaspoon of saline solution and stir well. Keep adding a teaspoon at a time of the saline solution. Stir for about 15 seconds each time you add the saline solution. You know it is ready when it holds together well but is still a loose slime. Now you can optionally stick the plastic sea creatures down into the goo. It will look like they are "swimming" in the "water." You can also take the slime out of the bowl and squish this crunchy goop in your hands. It has a fun, crunchy, beachy feel!

TIPS

For extra fun, add glitter in with the acrylic vase filler before you stir it all up.

☐ **Store in an airtight container.**

SPIDER EGG SACK

ADULT SUPERVISION   DO NOT EAT

Have you ever seen a spider egg sack? They are white, sticky things full of baby spiders! Creep out your best friend or favorite adult with this terrifying gooey mix of hidden spiders. Don't worry. You will know they are totally fake.

INGREDIENTS

1 Melted-Snowman Slime recipe (page 19), without the accessories

1 packet of plastic baby spiders (you can find these online or at a party shop)

WHAT YOU DO

Make the Melted-Snowman Slime, leaving it undecorated. Form the slime into a ball. Here is the fun part. Stick the baby spiders up into the goo far enough that they can't be seen. Hand the goo to a friend, and tell them they can play with it. Hear them scream when they find the nest of spiders!!

You can put a big spider on top of the goo, like it's protecting its eggs. You can also gross people out by leaving the "egg sack" out where people can see it. You might start a prank war with this one!

☐ **Store in an airtight container.**

DO NOT
EAT

TOOTH-PASTE SLIME

This slime is made with two ingredients that you probably already have at home. It has a different texture, but is easy, breezy and fun.

INGREDIENTS

½ cup (120 ml) thick, creamy shampoo

2 tbsp (30 ml) white toothpaste

1 tbsp (24 g) glitter (optional)

1 tbsp (4 g) gelatin mix in your favorite color (optional)

EQUIPMENT

Bowl

Spoon

WHAT YOU DO

Put the shampoo in a bowl. Add the toothpaste to the bowl. Now is when you can add the glitter if you want, but let's get real. It's glitter. Who doesn't want to add it?! You can now also add your favorite color of gelatin mix if you desire. Stir it together with a spoon for about 90 seconds. If it is too stiff, add more shampoo. If it is too runny, add more toothpaste. Stir for 30 more seconds. Place the bowl of slimy goo in the freezer for about 30 minutes. When you take it out, the slime should be thick, but not too sticky. Squish and squeeze the slime until it is normal temperature again. Now it's ready!

TIPS

☐ **Store in an airtight container.**

🕐 **Limited shelf life.**

BUTTER SLIME

ADULT SUPERVISION

DO NOT EAT

This slime gets its name not only because it uses butter, but also because of how buttery soft it feels when you squish it between your fingers. Kind of a combination between a slime and a dough, this goo is stretchy, but spreadable like butter should be.

INGREDIENTS

¼ cup (40 g) cornstarch

¼ cup (33 g) baby powder

½ cup (120 ml) creamy, thick shampoo

1 (4-oz [118-ml]) bottle white school glue

2 tbsp (30 ml) hand lotion

7 drops yellow food coloring

About ½ cup (60 g) shaving cream (eyeball it)

1 tbsp (15 ml) baby oil

1 cup (230 g) softened butter

1 tsp baking soda

2 tbsp (30 ml) saline solution (make sure it says buffered on the package)

EQUIPMENT

Bowl

Spoon

WHAT YOU DO

Put the cornstarch, baby powder and shampoo in a bowl. Stir it with the spoon until it forms a sticky dough. Add the glue, lotion, food coloring, shaving cream, baby oil and butter, and stir it all together. Now, stir in the baking soda.

Next is the tricky part. You want to add the saline solution a little bit at a time. If you use too much, the slime will be too hard. Keep stirring. If it is a little on the sticky side, add a little more baby powder. When it's right, take it out of the bowl. Squish and knead it in your hands until the buttery perfection is achieved. This is so buttery smooth, you won't want to put it down!

TIPS

Butter Slime can be stored at room temperature for 2 weeks. If you want to keep it longer, you can refrigerate it, but be sure to label it so no one eats it!

☐ **Store in an airtight container.**

🕐 **Limited shelf life.**

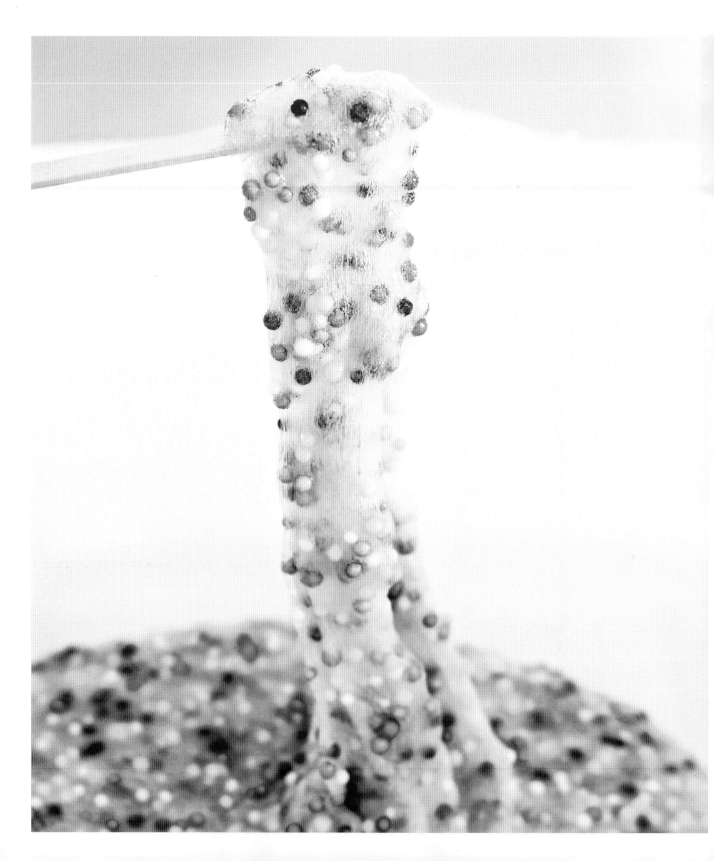

CRONCH SLIME

ADULT SUPERVISION

DO NOT EAT

What is cronch? It's like crunch, but so much better! Hear the crackle when you whip up a batch of this cool Cronch Slime. Your friends will be super jealous! They'll be begging you to make them some too!

INGREDIENTS

2 (5-oz [147-ml]) bottles clear school glue

1 tsp baking soda

1 cup (240 ml) warm water

1 (12-oz [355-ml]) bottle saline solution (make sure it says buffered on the package)

Bag of colored foam balls (bean-bag filler)

EQUIPMENT

Large glass mixing bowl

Spoon

Plastic craft tub

WHAT YOU DO

In the bowl, mix the two bottles of glue, the baking soda and the warm water. Mix until it's fully combined. Squirt about ½ teaspoon of the saline solution at a time into the glue mixture. Stir it vigorously, and give the solution time to react. Keep adding solution and stirring vigorously until the mixture starts to pull away from the sides of the bowl.

Now, mix for about 2 more minutes with the spoon. By this time, it should be ready to take out and knead, stretch and pull in your hands. Next, dump the bag of foam balls into the craft box. Place the slime you made into the container with the little balls. Squish and mush everything up until it is incorporated together. When you stretch and play with the slime, it should make a crunching sound.

TIPS

Use googly eyes (found at craft stores) instead of foam balls for a fun effect.

☐ **Store in an airtight container.**

CANDY SLIME

ADULT SUPERVISION

EDIBLE

A better name for this might be Laughing Slime. That's because it's made with Laffy Taffy® candy! Make a batch and bring on the rainbow giggles.

INGREDIENTS

1 bag of bite-size Laffy Taffy® candy (we used about 8 pieces of each color)

Water

FOR EACH COLOR OF CANDY

¼ tsp coconut oil

3 tbsp (24 g) powdered sugar

3 tbsp (30 g) cornstarch

EQUIPMENT

Bowls (for each color of candy)

Pot

Spoon

Plate

WHAT YOU DO

Unwrap and separate the Laffy Taffy® candy into the bowls by color. Get an adult to help you with the next part. Place a pot with 3 inches (7.6 cm) of water on the stove on medium-high heat. Place one of the bowls of candy into the water (basically using the double-boiler method), being careful not to get water on the candy so it doesn't seize. Heat up the candy until it is melted, stirring frequently. Once the candy is almost entirely melted, add the coconut oil and stir well.

While the adult is heating up the candy, place the powdered sugar and cornstarch on a plate. When the candy is done, have an adult take the bowl out of the water and pour the candy onto the plate with the cornstarch and sugar. Be careful. It will be hot. When the candy on the plate cools down enough to touch, knead and squish the candy into the cornstarch and sugar. Repeat with the remaining candy colors. You now have a rainbow of edible slimy goodness that smells great too!

TIPS

If the candy gets too tough again, have an adult pop it in the microwave and heat it for about 10 seconds. It will soften it up again. Save the wrappers to tell the jokes while you play with your candy slime.

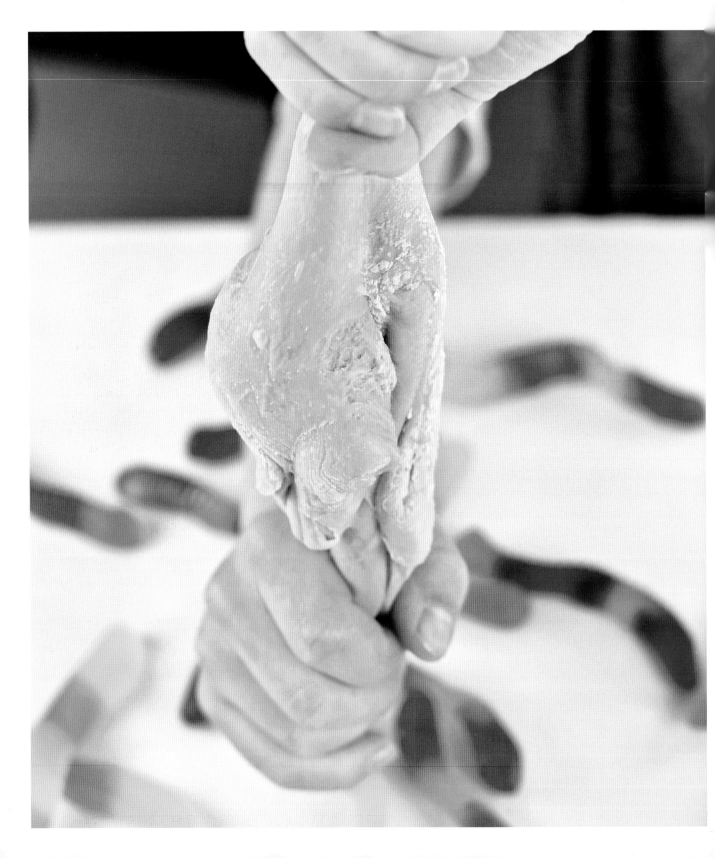

EDIBLE GUMMY WORM SLIME

Let's make worm slime! Eww. How about gummy worm slime? This recipe is going to wiggle its way right into your play (and tummy) when you make this edible slime!

INGREDIENTS

1½ cups (273 g) gummy worms

1 tsp vegetable oil

2 tbsp (20 g) cornstarch

2 tbsp (16 g) powdered sugar

EQUIPMENT

Microwave-safe bowl

Spoon

WHAT YOU DO

Make a pile with all the gummy worms inside your microwave-safe bowl. Ask an adult to microwave the bowl on high for 15-second increments until all of the gummy worms are melted. Stir with the spoon after each 15-second increment. Be careful. The bowl and candy will be hot. Add the vegetable oil and stir until combined. Mix the cornstarch and powdered sugar into the candy mixture until well combined. Allow the slime to cool. Now you have a smushy, tasty, stretchy treat you can nibble on while you play.

TIPS

If you find your slime sticky, you can add more cornstarch.

☐ **Store in an airtight container.**

FLUFFY SLIME

ADULT SUPERVISION

DO NOT EAT

This slime is so fluffy, it's almost like playing with pillowy billows of whipped cream. You'll be tempted to taste a bit of this soft cream. Resist the urge! Your taste buds won't love it as much as your hands do.

INGREDIENTS

1 (11-oz [311-g]) can shaving cream

1 packet powdered drink mix in your favorite color

1 (4-oz [118-ml]) bottle white school glue

1 tsp baking soda

1½ tbsp (23 ml) saline solution (make sure it says buffered on the package), divided

EQUIPMENT

Plastic tub

Spoon

WHAT YOU DO

Dump the shaving cream, drink mix and glue into a plastic craft tub. Fold this together with a spoon. Add the baking soda to the mix and keep folding.

Now, add a tablespoon (15 ml) of the saline solution to the mix, and start whipping it up! You might need an extra ½ tablespoon (8 ml) of saline solution if it is not coming together properly. Now, add a small amount of saline solution to your hands and knead the fluffy mixture on a flat surface. Have fun playing with this billowy soft, slimy goo!

TIPS

What is folding? Folding something together means mixing it up carefully by bringing the bottom of the mix up to the top and repeating.

☐ **Store in an airtight container.**

EDIBLE RED LICORICE SLIME

ADULT SUPERVISION

EDIBLE

Red licorice is one of those timeless candies that everyone has tried at least once. This classic sweet berry flavor is just screaming to get its turn as a slime. At last! Your imagination, and taste buds, will jump for joy.

INGREDIENTS

1 cup (182 g) cut red licorice

1 tsp coconut oil

1 tsp raspberry gelatin powder

1 tbsp (8 g) powdered sugar

1 tsp cornstarch

EQUIPMENT

Kitchen scissors

Microwave-safe bowl

Spoon

Small bowl

WHAT YOU DO

With an adult's help, use the kitchen scissors to cut the red licorice into small pieces. Place the pieces of candy in the microwave-safe bowl. Add the coconut oil to the candy. Microwave for 20-second intervals, stirring after each interval using the spoon. When the mixture is melted, have an adult take the bowl out of the microwave. Be careful! It will be hot. Let the mixture cool down a bit. In a small bowl, mix together the gelatin, powdered sugar and cornstarch. Add it to the bowl of melted licorice. Stir vigorously with the spoon until well combined. After the mixture is completely cool, you can pick it up. Throw it down on a flat surface. Knead it, stretch it, eat it.

TIPS

☐ **Store in an airtight container.**

🕐 **Limited shelf life.**

RED HOT TAMALE SLIME

ADULT SUPERVISION

DO NOT EAT

Red, glittery slime is taken to an entirely new level with the scent of red-hot cinnamon. Easy to make, and so good to smell, this goop just might be the perfect slime.

INGREDIENTS

½ cup (99 g) Hot Tamale® candy

½ tsp coconut oil

1 (5-oz [147-ml]) bottle clear school glue

5 drops red food coloring

1 tbsp (24 g) red glitter

¼ cup (60 ml) hot (not boiling) water

½ tsp baking soda

1 tbsp (15 ml) saline solution (make sure it says buffered on the package)

EQUIPMENT

Microwave-safe bowl

Spoon

WHAT YOU DO

Put the candy and the coconut oil into your bowl. With an adult's help, put the bowl in the microwave. Microwave it for 20 seconds at a time, stirring well each time it's done. Be careful! It will get hot! It is done when it is a thick liquid mixture. Let it cool down for 3 minutes.

Add the bottle of glue, your food coloring and the glitter to the candy. Mix well with the spoon. Add the water and the baking soda. Add the saline solution, a little at a time, to the mixture. Stir well the entire time. It is done when the mixture starts to pull away from the sides of the bowl. Take out your goo. Knead it, poke it and stretch it until it is not as sticky. You now have a delicious-smelling red slime!

TIPS

☐ **Store in an airtight container.**

🕐 **Limited shelf life.**

SPIDERWEB SLIME

ADULT SUPERVISION

DO NOT EAT

Real spiderwebs start as a simple thread made by a spider. They turn this plain little piece of thread into uberfancy works of spider art. You do not need the creepy-crawly spider to make your supercool spider web! You just need this webby slime.

INGREDIENTS

1 (4-oz [118-ml]) bottle white school glue

1 cup (240 ml) foaming hand soap

½ tbsp (8 ml) creamy shower gel or shampoo

½ tbsp (8 ml) hand lotion

½ tbsp (8 ml) baby oil

2½ heaping cups (300 g) shaving cream, plus more for spreading

1 to 2 tbsp (15 to 30 ml) liquid starch (you can find this in the laundry aisle)

EQUIPMENT

Large mixing bowl

Spoon

Airtight container

WHAT YOU DO

Fold the glue, soap, gel or shampoo, lotion, baby oil and shaving cream together in a bowl. Add the liquid starch a little at a time, folding it together the entire time. Now, get in there with your hands and knead, squeeze and fold that goo. It will be very sticky at first, but will eventually start to pull away from the sides of the bowl.

Now, take out that slime, and put it on a clean, flat surface. Play with, poke and knead this semi-sticky substance for about 15 minutes. It should be the consistency of a puffy slime. Put the slime in an airtight container. Using your hands, spread a thin layer of shaving cream over the top of the slime. Cover the container tightly with a lid. Let it sit for 2 to 3 days. When you take off the lid, the slime will look like spiderwebs and be crackly and crunchy. Push, poke and fold the slime in the container. This slime is so much fun!

TIPS

Add 6 drops of food coloring in the first step to give the slime a pop of color.

To make it foamier, add ½ cup (60 g) more of shaving cream in the first step.

☐ Store in an airtight container.

🕐 Limited shelf life.

SNOW CONE SLIME

Did you say snow cone? Yes, please! What's better than chilling with a deliciously colorful snow cone on a hot summer day? Why, making one that doesn't melt of course!

INGREDIENTS

1 (5-oz [147-ml]) bottle clear glue

1½ tsp (8 ml) liquid starch (you can find this in the laundry aisle)

2 cups (400 g) polypropylene plastic pellets (you can find them at a craft store)

Food coloring (optional)

Food extract (optional)

EQUIPMENT

Small bowl

Airtight container

Mixing bowl

Spoon

Paper cones found at party stores (optional)

WHAT YOU DO

Mix the glue and starch in a small bowl very gently. You might want to let the mixture sit in an airtight container for about 3 to 4 days to become completely clear. When it's ready, place the slime in a mixing bowl. Add the plastic pellets ¼ cup (50 g) at a time, squishing them into the slime. The slime will eventually turn crackly and it will become harder to add the pellets. When you are done, you will have what looks like a crunchy snow cone.

TIPS

Add your favorite color of food coloring to make it look like your favorite snow cone.

Add your favorite-smelling food extract to make it smell yummy.

Squish the mixture into paper cones (found at party stores) to really give it that snow cone look.

DO NOT EAT THIS SNOW CONE. It looks amazing, but is not edible.

☐ Store in an airtight container.

HOLOGRAPHIC SLIME

ADULT SUPERVISION

DO NOT EAT

Three-dimensional rainbows of color you can hold in your hand: that is what this slime is all about! Get hypnotized by the color spectrum you'll create with this slimy masterpiece.

INGREDIENTS

1 (5-oz [147-ml]) bottle clear school glue

½ cup (120 ml) water

2 tbsp (48 g) holographic powder or glitter

1 tbsp (15 ml) white acrylic paint

½ tsp baking soda

2 tbsp (30 ml) saline solution (make sure it says buffered on the package)

EQUIPMENT

Bowl

Spoon

WHAT YOU DO

Pour the glue, water, powder or glitter, paint and baking soda into a bowl, and mix up the solution until it is well combined. Add the saline solution a little at a time, stirring with each addition, until the mixture starts to pull away from the bowl. Take out the goopy, shiny slime, and place it on a flat surface. Okay, now you can play with your holographic slime!

TIPS

Use glow-in-the-dark paint instead of white paint to see the sparkles even when it's dark. It's such a fun way to play with this slime.

☐ **Store in an airtight container.**

ADULT
SUPERVISION

DO NOT
EAT

LAUNDRY SOAP SLIME

Can slime really be this easy? Yes! You probably already have these ingredients in your home. This is a good slime to start with if you are new to the slime game. It is so simple!

INGREDIENTS

1 (5-oz [147-ml]) bottle clear school glue

½ cup (120 ml) liquid laundry soap (Tide® works best)

EQUIPMENT

Bowl

Spoon

WHAT YOU DO

Pour the glue into the bowl. Add a teaspoon at a time of laundry soap, stirring well each time you add it. Keep adding detergent and stirring until the mixture pulls away from the sides of the bowl. Voila! You have Laundry Soap Slime.

TIPS

Add 1 tablespoon (24 g) of your favorite color of glitter if desired.

Add 2 drops of food coloring to change the color.

Store in an airtight container.

CONTACT SLIME

DO NOT EAT

This is another easy slime recipe, and it also doubles as a science experiment! What makes the contact solution turn the baking soda and glue into squishable slime? It has to do with how the polymers bond to one another. I bet you didn't think you were going to be a scientist today!

INGREDIENTS

1 (4-oz [118-ml]) bottle white school glue

1 tsp baking soda

1 tbsp (15 ml) saline solution (make sure it says buffered on the package)

EQUIPMENT

Bowl

Spoon

WHAT YOU DO

Put the glue in your bowl. Add the baking soda and stir the mixture together. Add the contact solution (also known as saline) a little at a time, stirring while you add. When the slime starts to pull away from the sides of the bowl, it is ready. You can now take it out and play! The more you squish it with your hands, the better it will become.

TIPS

Add 2 drops of food coloring for fun, colorful play.

Add 2 teaspoons (16 g) of glitter for some sparkly amazingness.

☐ **Store in an airtight container.**

COKE® SLIME

Some call it Coke®. Some call it soda pop or just soda. Whatever you call it, this fizzy beverage will make an awesome-smelling slime that is hard to resist.

INGREDIENTS

1 cup (240 ml) Coca-Cola®

1½ tsp (14 g) borax powder

1 (5-oz [147-ml]) bottle clear school glue

EQUIPMENT

Bowl

Spoon

WHAT YOU DO

Mix the Coca-Cola® and borax powder in the bowl. Be careful, the borax will make the Coca-Cola® fizzy. Add the glue and stir the mixture together. Keep stirring until the slime pulls away from the sides of the bowl. Now, get your hands in there and mix it together. The more you play with it, knead it, roll it and fold it with your hands, the less sticky it will be.

TIPS

Add a tablespoon (24 g) of glitter to the mix as you stir it. This will give your slime a pop of bling.

Try this with different soda pops to get different yummy scents.

☐ **Store in an airtight container.**

GLITTER GLUE SLIME

ADULT SUPERVISION

DO NOT EAT

When you think of glitter glue, you probably think of fun crafts that involve adding a sparkle to your art. This same glue can be used to make a twinkling slime. With just a few ingredients, you can turn a bottle of crafty glitter glue into an ooey, gooey slime that you can stretch, pull and play with.

INGREDIENTS

1 (6-oz [177-ml]) bottle glitter glue

5 drops matching food coloring (optional)

¼ tsp borax powder

½ cup (120 ml) warm water

EQUIPMENT

2 bowls

Spoon

WHAT YOU DO

Pour the glitter glue into a bowl. Mix in the food coloring, if desired, to give your slime a more vibrant color.

In the second bowl, mix the borax powder into the warm water until it dissolves. Fold this mixture into the glue a bit at a time. It is ready when the slime pulls away from the sides of the bowl. Get your hands ready, and grab the glob of goo out of the bowl. Smoosh it between your fingers, pull it apart with your hands and play with it on a flat surface. The more you play with it, the less sticky it will become.

TIPS

You may not use all of the borax-water solution. Discard any unused solution.

☐ **Store in an airtight container.**

◇ **Refresh with water.**

KINETIC SLIME

ADULT SUPERVISION

DO NOT EAT

This slime has a jiggle and feels snotty, like the goo you know and love. It also holds itself together unlike any slime you've ever played with. Just wait until you feel this mix for yourself! You will become an addict of the kinetic craze.

INGREDIENTS

1½ cups (551 g) play sand (you can find this at a craft or hardware store)

2 tbsp (20 g) cornstarch

1½ tbsp (23 ml) of your favorite liquid hand soap

½ tbsp (8 ml) coconut oil

1 (4-oz [118-ml]) bottle white school glue

½ cup (120 ml) liquid starch (you can find this in the laundry aisle)

EQUIPMENT

Plastic craft bin

Bowl

Spoon

WHAT YOU DO

Pour the play sand, cornstarch, soap and coconut oil into the plastic bin. Mix it all up with your hands. Set it aside.

Pour the bottle of glue into the bowl. Add a little bit of the liquid starch at a time. Keep stirring the entire time. When the mixture starts to pull away from the sides of the bowl, it's done.

Take it out of the bowl, and mix and knead it with your hands until it isn't so sticky and you have a good slime. Add the slime into the sand mixture in the plastic bin. Using your hands, squish the whole thing into one big blob of kinetic slime. This may take some time, but be patient. This slime is amazeballs!

TIP

☐ **Store in an airtight container.**

PUFFY CLOUD SLIME

ADULT SUPERVISION

DO NOT EAT

Look up at the sky and what do you see? Clouds you wish you could grab and squish in your hands. With this superfoamy slime, it's almost like you are plucking those billowy puffs right out of the sky. Grab some and squish away!

INGREDIENTS

1 cup (240 ml) white school glue

3 pumps of hand lotion

2 pumps of foaming hand soap

1 tbsp (10 g) cornstarch

½ tsp borax

1 cup (240 ml) water

EQUIPMENT

2 bowls

Spoon

WHAT YOU DO

Mix the glue, lotion, soap and cornstarch in a bowl until combined. You should have a foam-like mixture.

In a separate bowl, dissolve the borax in the water. Add the borax solution to the glue a little at a time, stirring, until your slime starts to form and pull away from the sides of the bowl.

Knead it and play with it until it is slimy but doesn't stick to your hands. Now you have your super excellent cloud slime.

TIP

☐ Store in an airtight container.

ICEBERG SLIME

ADULT SUPERVISION

DO NOT EAT

What is an iceberg? It is a ginormous piece of ice, sometimes as big as an island, that has broken off a glacier. This hard piece of giant ice floats around in the open ocean. Make a bit of "iceberg" in your own home using this slime recipe that hardens as it sits.

INGREDIENTS

1 (4-oz [118-ml]) bottle white school glue

1 (11-oz [311-g]) can shaving cream

2 tbsp (30 ml) hand lotion

2 tbsp (16 g) baby powder

1 packet powdered drink mix in your favorite color

1 tsp borax powder

1 cup (240 ml) hot (not boiling) water

EQUIPMENT

Spoon

Large plastic mixing bowl or plastic bin

Smaller bowl

Rubber mallet or hammer

WHAT YOU DO

Using a spoon, mix the glue, shaving cream, lotion, baby powder and drink mix together in the large mixing bowl until fully combined. Mix the borax powder and water together in the smaller bowl using a spoon. Add the borax-water solution into the large bowl of goo, a little at a time, stirring each time to fully incorporate. When you are finished, it should nicely pull away from the sides of the bowl.

Dump the poufy goo onto a clean, flat surface. Knead it, fold it, poke it and play with it for about 15 minutes. Drop the puff of play goo back into the large bowl. Put the bowl in a safe place. Let it sit, uncovered, for 3 days.

When the time is up, feel the top. It should be hard and crunchy. With the help of an adult, use the mallet or hammer to crack the surface of your homemade "iceberg." When you are done breaking up the surface, you can fold and play with the goo until it is all soft and fluffy again. Now you can put it back in the bowl, and start hardening your "iceberg" again!

CLOUD SLIME

ADULT SUPERVISION

DO NOT EAT

You know how in the winter it sometimes just feels like snow? You can tell it is up there in the clouds, but it hasn't fallen to the ground yet. That is exactly how this slime is! It is a puffy cloud full of "snow" that you can actually have fun with in your hands!

INGREDIENTS

3 tbsp (36 g) instant snow powder (you can find this at a craft store or online)

3 cups (720 ml) water, divided

1 tsp borax

1 (4-oz [118-ml]) bottle white school glue

6 drops of your favorite food coloring (optional)

3 drops peppermint oil (optional)

EQUIPMENT

Large craft tub

Cup

Spoon

Bowl

WHAT YOU DO

Dump the snow powder into your craft tub. Add about 2 cups (480 ml) of water. This "snow" will grow as you add the water. Set that aside.

Now, grab your cup. Add 1 cup (240 ml) of water and your borax to the cup. Stir this mixture until it is completely dissolved. Empty your bottle of glue into the bowl. Next, mix your food coloring and peppermint oil in with the glue if you desire. Slowly add your borax mixture, about a teaspoon at a time, to the glue. Mix well after each time you add the borax mixture. The goo is ready when it starts to pull away from the sides of the bowl.

Take it out of the bowl, and knead, stretch and pull it until it isn't quite so sticky anymore. Now, throw this goo into your tub of snow. Knead the snow into the slime really well. Play with it until the slime is full of the snow, and none of it is falling out. You will not use all of the snow. Now you have made your perfect cloud slime!

TIP

☐ **Store in an airtight container.**

GUMMY BEAR SLIME

ADULT SUPERVISION

EDIBLE

Yum. Squish. Yum. Squish. Stretch. Play. Repeat. This slime is made with completely edible ingredients, and you won't find a tastier glob to stretch your imagination.

INGREDIENTS

1½ cups (273 g) gummy bears

1 tsp vegetable oil

1 tsp gelatin in your favorite flavor

2½ tbsp (20 g) powdered sugar

2½ tbsp (25 g) cornstarch

EQUIPMENT

Microwave-safe bowl

Spoon

WHAT YOU DO

Pile the gummy bears into the bowl. Drizzle the vegetable oil over the gummy bears. With an adult's help, put the bowl into the microwave. Microwave in 20-second increments, stirring after each time. When the gummy bears have turned to a liquid consistency, have an adult take the bowl out of the microwave. Be careful. It will be hot. Let it cool down a little, then stir in your flavored gelatin, the powdered sugar and the cornstarch with a spoon. If it's too runny, add more sugar. If it's too firm, add a bit more oil. When it's done, it should be stretchy, tacky and edible!

TIPS

☐ **Store in an airtight container.**

🕐 **Limited shelf life.**

FUZZY SLIME MONSTER

ADULT SUPERVISION

DO NOT EAT

Not all monsters are scary. They can be cute, ooey and gooey too. What will your monster become once you finish this supercool recipe? It's your monster. You decide!

INGREDIENTS

1 (4-oz [118-ml]) bottle white school glue

2 tbsp (30 ml) liquid starch

2 tsp (10 ml) of acrylic paint in your favorite color

2 tbsp (48 g) glitter (optional)

4 cotton balls, shredded

Googly eyes (different sizes are fun)

A few colorful play feathers (optional)

1 pipe cleaner, cut in 6 pieces (optional)

EQUIPMENT

Large bowl

Spoon

WHAT YOU DO

Pour the bottle of glue into the bowl, and slowly add in the starch while stirring. You may not need all 2 tablespoons (30 ml). You want the slime to just release from the sides of the bowl. Add your acrylic paint and, if you like, glitter, and continue squishing the slime up until it is an even color.

Now, take the shredded cotton balls one at a time, and squeeze and fold them into the slime. When you are done, take your blob of "fuzzy" slime out of the bowl. Shape it into a glob monster. Add as many googly eyes as you want. If you desire, stick the colorful feathers in the top for hair. Use the pipe cleaners for arms, horns, a nose or whatever else your imagination creates. It's your Fuzzy Slime Monster!

TIPS

The pipe cleaners can be a bit pokey once cut. Use with care.

☐ **Store in an airtight container.**

GOOGLY EYE SLIME

ADULT SUPERVISION   DO NOT EAT

What's that you see peering at you through a haze of goo? Could it be your squishy, slithery slime? It just might be! The more eyes, the more fun with this glob of superjiggly fun.

INGREDIENTS

1 cup (240 ml) hot water

1 tbsp (27 g) borax

1 (5-oz [147-ml]) bottle clear school glue

2 tbsp (30 ml) water

¼ cup (50 g) googly eyes

EQUIPMENT

2 bowls

Spoon

WHAT YOU DO

Ask an adult to help you mix the hot water and the borax in a bowl with a spoon until the borax is completely dissolved. Set it to the side. Pour the glue into the second bowl. Gently mix in the 2 tablespoons (30 ml) of water to thin the glue out. Try not to get too many air bubbles into the mix. Pour the glue mixture into the borax mixture. Slowly stir the glue around in the water for about 30 seconds. Let the mixture sit for about 5 minutes.

When the time is up, take the slime out of the water. Flatten it out with your hands on a clean, dry surface. Add the googly eyes to the center of the slime. Fold the slime up around the googly eyes. Now, squish it all together until it's combined. When the eyes are peering in all directions out of the slime, you know it's ready!

TIP ☐ **Store in an airtight container.**

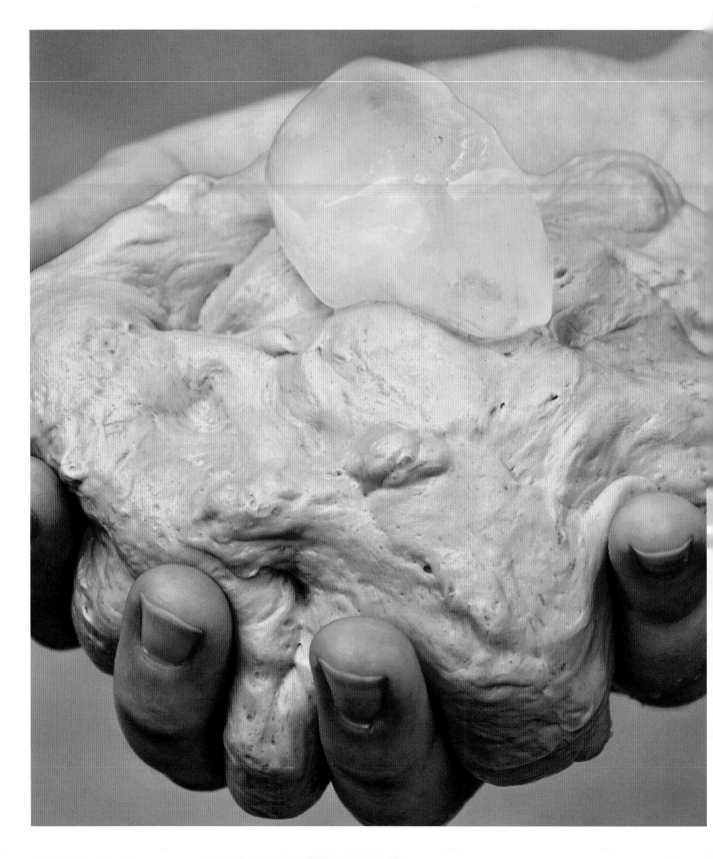

COLOR-CHANGING SLIME

ADULT SUPERVISION

DO NOT EAT

Is it pink? Is it black? It just might be both! With the thermochromic pigment found in this recipe, temperature can determine the color of your slime. How does that even work?!

INGREDIENTS

1 (4-oz [118-ml]) bottle white school glue

2 to 3 tsp (30 to 46 g) thermochromic pigment (you can find this online)

½ tsp baking soda

1 cup (120 g) shaving cream

1 tbsp (15 ml) hand lotion

1 tsp baby powder

1 tbsp (15 ml) saline solution (make sure it says buffered on the package)

EQUIPMENT

Bowl

Spoon

WHAT YOU DO

Add the glue to the bowl. Sprinkle in the thermochromatic pigment. Be careful: This can be messy. Once it is all mixed up, stir in the baking soda.

To make it fluffy, add the shaving cream, folding it into the mixture until it is all incorporated. Now, fold in the lotion and baby powder. Add the saline solution in small amounts, stirring vigorously after each addition. You may not need the full amount, or you might need a little more. The more you add, the more tough the mixture will become. Now, take out the blob of goo. Knead it in your hands until it is no longer sticky. You will want to play with this one forever!

TIPS

Warm your hands up by blowing on them or rubbing them together before you play with the slime. More heat equals more color change.

Rub ice along the surface of the slime. Colder temperatures equal more color change.

☐ **Store in an airtight container.**

ADULT
SUPERVISION

DO NOT
EAT

GLOSSY SLIME

Isn't all slime a bit glossy? This slime is *extra* glossy. It almost shines with a blingy luster as you squeeze, pull, twist and play.

INGREDIENTS

1 (4-oz [118-ml]) bottle white school glue

2 tbsp (30 ml) baby oil

2 tsp (6 g) baby powder

2 tsp (10 ml) water

6 drops food coloring (optional)

¼ cup (60 ml) liquid laundry detergent

EQUIPMENT

Bowl

Spoon

WHAT YOU DO

Put the glue and baby oil in the bowl and mix well. Add the baby powder and water. Mix up the ingredients until a soft dough forms. Add the food coloring, if desired, and mix until it's evenly blended. Now, add the laundry detergent a little at a time, stirring vigorously each time you add more detergent. The slime will be ready when it pulls away from the sides of the bowl. Take the slime out of the bowl. Knead and stretch it until it is no longer sticky.

TIPS

Put a tiny bit of baby oil on your hands before you play with the slime. This will keep it from sticking.

☐ **Store in an airtight container.**

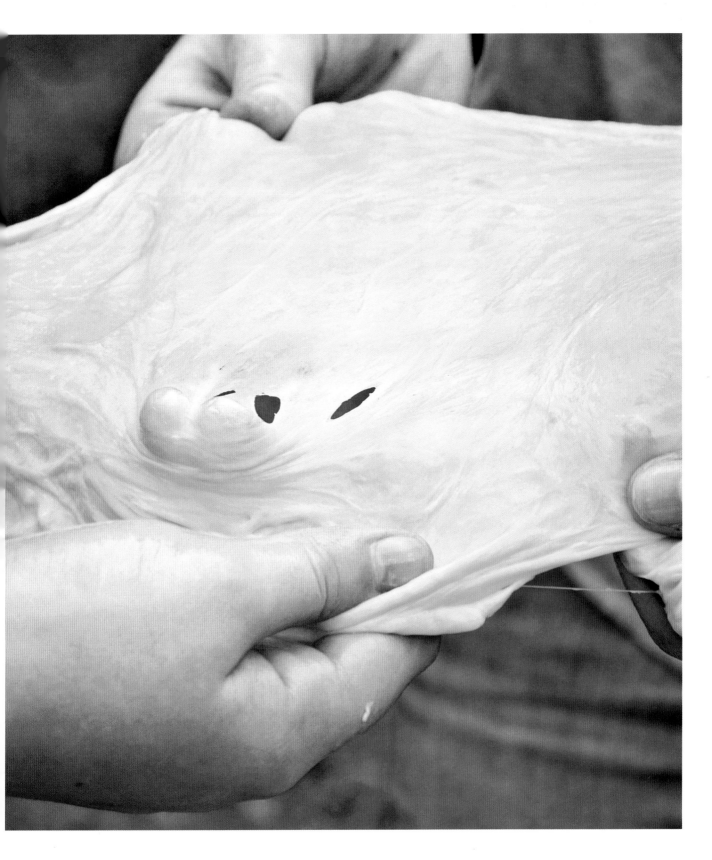

CHEETAH SLIME

ADULT SUPERVISION

DO NOT EAT

What's black and orange and super fast? A cheetah, of course. So is this slimy mixture. Fast to make, that is. Have your own cheetah fun in under 10 minutes!

INGREDIENTS

1 (5-oz [147-ml]) bottle clear school glue

2 tbsp (30 ml) liquid starch (you can find this in the laundry aisle)

10 drops orange food coloring (or mix yellow and red)

¼ cup (200 g) small black sequence beads

EQUIPMENT

Bowl

Spoon

WHAT YOU DO

Empty your entire bottle of glue into a bowl. Gently stir the liquid starch into the glue. Try not to "whip" the mixture. You want as little air in the mixture as possible. Add in your food coloring and keep stirring. The slime is ready when it starts pulling away from the bowl. Add in your sequence beads, squishing and kneading until the beads are evenly dispersed. Now you have cool Cheetah Slime!

TIP ☐ **Store in an airtight container.**

CLEAR SLIME

This clear slime recipe is a great base for so many slime recipes. Whether you add to it or play with it as is, this slime is wicked cool! It almost looks like you are playing with and shaping water. Your friends will be a bit confused, and totally amazed.

INGREDIENTS

½ cup (120 ml) hot water

¼ tsp borax

1 (5-oz [147-ml]) bottle clear school glue

½ cup (120 ml) room-temperature water

EQUIPMENT

2 bowls

Spoon

WHAT YOU DO

Ask an adult to help you mix the hot water and the borax in a bowl until the borax is completely dissolved. Set it to the side.

Pour the glue in the second bowl. Gently mix in the ½ cup (120 ml) of room-temperature water to thin the glue out. Try not to get too many air bubbles into the mix.

Pour the glue mixture into the borax mixture. Slowly stir the glue around in the water for about 30 seconds. Let the mixture sit for about 5 minutes. When the time is up, knead the slime in the borax solution for about a minute more. Take the slime out. Stretch it out and hold it up. You should be able to see right through it!

TIPS

Be sure to throw out any unused borax solution.

Store in an airtight container.

PLAYDOUGH

These dough activities are all about the squish.
They're fun to smoosh and moosh and you can even use
them to sculpt and design. Some of these doughs are all natural,
and some of them are made from cake frosting, but all of these
doughs are ridiculously cool! You can mix different colors
and textures together to make pretty much
anything you want!

THE BEST HOMEMADE PLAYDOUGH

ADULT SUPERVISION

Want a smooshy, fun-to-make alternative to store-bought dough? You are bound to get hours of laughs and giggles from this fun dough. It is the world's best homemade playdough.

INGREDIENTS

2 cups (240 g) flour

½ cup (137 g) salt

2 tbsp (10 g) cream of tartar

2 tbsp (30 ml) oil (any kitchen oil will do—coconut oil, vegetable oil, even olive oil)

1½ cups (360 ml) boiling water

Food coloring (optional)

EQUIPMENT

Large bowl

Spoon

WHAT YOU DO

Pour the flour, salt and cream of tartar into a large bowl. Stir in the kitchen oil of your choice. Have an adult help you pour the boiling water very carefully into the bowl. Be careful! It will be very hot. Mix all the ingredients together with a spoon until you get dough. Let it cool completely, and then make a ball with the dough. Now, punch the middle of the ball to make a hole. Put a few drops of food coloring in the hole you made, if you like. Knead the ball with your hands until it is all mixed together. Now you have your homemade playdough!

TIPS

Gel food coloring makes more vibrant colors than regular liquid food coloring.

While you are kneading the color into the dough, it can stain your hands. Wear plastic gloves to prevent this. Keep the dough in the bowl to keep it from staining surfaces.

☐ **Store in an airtight container.**

◌ **Refresh with water.**

HOT CHOCOLATE PLAYDOUGH

ADULT SUPERVISION

Hot chocolate is just one of those things that makes everyone feel happy, relaxed and ready to hang out. This hot chocolate playdough is just the thing to pull out on a cold winter day. For extra fun, pair it with our Marshmallow Playdough (page 82) and stick it in a mug to make it look like real hot chocolate!

INGREDIENTS

2 cups (480 ml) water

1½ cups (188 g) flour

4 (0.75-oz [21 g]) packets of hot chocolate mix

1 cup (273 g) salt

2 to 3 tbsp (30 to 45 ml) vegetable oil

EQUIPMENT

Saucepan

Spoon

Wax paper

WHAT YOU DO

Ask an adult to mix the water, flour, hot chocolate mix, salt and vegetable oil over low heat in a saucepan and stir for about a minute until the dough is formed. Let your dough cool and pull it out of the saucepan onto wax paper. Knead the dough together until it is fully mixed. This dough will make your whole home smell as good as hot chocolate tastes!

TIPS

If your dough is too oily, just add an extra packet of hot cocoa.

☐ **Store in an airtight container.**

🕐 **Limited shelf life.**

MARSH-MALLOW PLAYDOUGH

ADULT SUPERVISION   EDIBLE

Making Marshmallow Playdough is as much fun as it sounds. It's even okay to put in your mouth! This can get sticky and gooey if you play with it for too long at one time, but that's half the fun!

INGREDIENTS

¾ cup (35 g) miniature marshmallows

2 tsp (10 ml) vegetable oil (or olive or coconut oil)

6 to 7 drops food coloring (optional)

5 to 6 tbsp (50 to 60 g) cornstarch

EQUIPMENT

Large microwave-safe bowl (a big one! Marshmallows expand when they're hot!)

Spoon

WHAT YOU DO

With an adult's help, put your marshmallows and oil into the microwave-safe bowl and heat for about 30 seconds. If you're using food coloring, you'll want to add it now. Stir well and return the bowl to the microwave. You're basically heating everything up until the marshmallows start to get big. When it's done, have an adult take the bowl out of the microwave and add some of the cornstarch. Stir, and keep adding until your playdough is not too sticky. This is going to make a stretchy playdough that is taste-safe!

TIPS

If your dough is too sticky, just add more cornstarch. You can also use colored marshmallows instead of food coloring; just be sure to separate the colors before heating each of them.

☐ **Store in an airtight container.**

🕐 **Limited shelf life.**

ICE CREAM DOUGH

ADULT SUPERVISION

EDIBLE

This dough looks exactly like ice cream. One of our favorite ways to play with it is to get a couple of scoops and add it to some real waffle cones. If you want to make it even more fun, you can add in a few sundae toppings for a super treat!

INGREDIENTS

1 (6.4-oz [181-g]) can premade frosting (get a fun color!)

6 cups (780 g) powdered sugar

Waffle cones

EQUIPMENT

Mixing bowl

Mixer

Ice cream scoops

WHAT YOU DO

Dump all of your frosting into the mixing bowl and start the mixer. Now, slowly pour in the powdered sugar and let the ingredients combine. Pull out your dough and scoop it onto the waffle cones for some silly, doughy fun!

TIPS

If your dough is crumbly, add a little oil to make it stretchy again!

☐ Store in an airtight container.

🕐 Limited shelf life.

ADULT SUPERVISION

DO NOT EAT

CRACKED-EGG DOUGH

Want to freak out your friends? This dough looks almost exactly like a real egg! You get to create a slimy, doughy, clear goo surrounding a yellow "yolk" of dough. Have your friends open one and hear them gasp and giggle!

INGREDIENTS

1 ball of Clear Playdough (page 93)

1 yellow ball of The Best Homemade Playdough (page 78)

EQUIPMENT

2 bowls

2 bags of plastic fillable Easter eggs

WHAT YOU DO

Place the Clear Playdough in one bowl. Make little balls about the size of egg yolks with the yellow Homemade Playdough. Do this by rolling the dough around in your hands. Place the yellow balls you create in your second bowl.

Open one of the plastic Easter eggs. Fill one half of the egg with Clear Playdough. Squish one of the yellow balls into the clear doughy goo. Fill the other half of the egg with Clear Playdough. Place the two halves of the egg together and close it. Repeat with all your plastic eggs.

This can get messy. Make these fun eggs over a table or other hard play surface.

☐ **Store in an airtight container.**

🕐 **Limited shelf life.**

CAKE BATTER DOUGH

EDIBLE

Cake batter has a crazy feel to it that's hard to explain, but this dough looks and feels just like it! This is the perfect project to pull out when Mom or Dad is baking in the kitchen and wants to keep little hands busy!

INGREDIENTS

1 cup (108 g) confetti cake mix

2 tbsp (14 g) premade confetti frosting (with sprinkles)

1 tbsp (10 g) cornstarch

1 cup (176 g) sprinkles

EQUIPMENT

Bowl

Spoon

WHAT YOU DO

In a bowl, combine your cake mix and frosting. Stir well. Add the cornstarch a little at a time until it becomes less sticky. The more you knead it, the more it will become like dough. Once you reach the consistency you like, add in the sprinkles. You can then play with the dough and even use cookie cutters to cut out fun shapes!

TIPS

If your dough is too sticky, just add more cornstarch.

☐ **Store in an airtight container.**

🕑 **Limited shelf life.**

LAVENDER PLAYDOUGH

ADULT SUPERVISION

DO NOT EAT

Sometimes you just need to chill out and squish something. This lavender playdough is exactly perfect for that. The smell is naturally calming, and the sprigs give it a textured crunchy feel!

INGREDIENTS

1¼ cups (300 ml) water

1 cup (273 g) salt

2 tbsp (30 ml) vegetable oil

2 tbsp (20 g) cream of tartar

2 cups (250 g) flour

Sprigs of lavender

EQUIPMENT

Saucepan

Bowl

Spoon

WHAT YOU DO

With an adult's help, boil the water in a saucepan. While that is cooking, add the salt, oil, cream of tartar and flour to the bowl and mix them together. Your adult can then pour the boiling water into the mixture and stir it with the spoon until it forms into a ball. Let it cool a bit. Once cool, pull the ball out of the bowl and drop it onto the counter. Knead it with your hands until the dough forms. Take your lavender and sprinkle the flower petals into the dough. Fold the petals into the mixture, and you have a nice calming dough for when you just need some chill time!

TIPS

If your dough is sticky, sprinkle in some more flour. If your dough is too dry, you can add a little more water or oil.

☐ **Store in an airtight container.**

🕐 **Limited shelf life.**

SOFTEST PLAYDOUGH

DO NOT
EAT

When you think of something being soft, you don't usually think of playdough, but this playdough is so soft and silky you won't ever want to play with anything else.

INGREDIENTS

1 cup (240 ml) white lotion (can be scented or unscented)

2½ cups (400 g) cornstarch

Food coloring

EQUIPMENT

Large bowl

WHAT YOU DO

In a large bowl, mix together the lotion, cornstarch and a few drops of food coloring. Use your hands to knead the ingredients together until you form the softest, smoothest dough ever!

TIPS

If the mixture is sticky, add a bit more cornstarch.

☐ Store in an airtight container.

NATURALLY-DYED PLAYDOUGH

ADULT SUPERVISION

Before there was ever food coloring in a tube or jar, people used natural things like fruits, flowers and spices to change the color of foods. We can do that same thing with playdough, changing its color without ever having to use any dye!

INGREDIENTS

30 blueberries

1 cup (240 ml) water

½ cup (63 g) flour

¼ cup (68 g) salt

½ tbsp (5 g) cream of tartar

½ tbsp (8 ml) vegetable oil

EQUIPMENT

Saucepan

Paper towel

Bowl

Spoon

WHAT YOU DO

Have an adult put the blueberries and water into a saucepan on the stove and bring it to a boil. Reduce the heat and let the mixture simmer for 30 minutes, until it is a thick consistency. Leave it to cool for another 30 minutes, then place a paper towel over the bowl and pour the mixture through it and into the bowl, catching all the parts you don't want in your dough. This should leave you with a very deep blue-purple water. That is how you will dye your dough!

Next, combine all the flour, salt, cream of tartar and vegetable oil in a saucepan with ½ cup (120 ml) of dyed water and ask an adult to stir it on low heat until the mixture rolls up into a ball. Let it cool just enough so that it won't burn your hands and drop it on your kitchen counter. Knead it together until it's fully formed into dough!

TIPS

If your dough is sticky, sprinkle in some more flour. If your dough is too dry, you can add a little water or oil.

If you are concerned about counter-top staining, use parchment or wax paper.

☐ **Store in an airtight container.**

🕐 **Limited shelf life.**

ADULT SUPERVISION

DO NOT EAT

FEATHER DOUGH

This supereasy, feather-soft dough is a fun way for you to spend quality kitchen time with a grown-up. Whether you mold it, squish it, cut it or shape it, this four-ingredient dough is bound to bring you hours of fun.

INGREDIENTS

¼ cup (40 g) cornstarch

½ cup (81 g) baking soda

¼ cup plus 1 tbsp (75 ml) water

1 tbsp (15 ml) baby oil

Food coloring (optional)

EQUIPMENT

Small saucepan

Spoon

Parchment paper

WHAT YOU DO

In a small saucepan, stir together the cornstarch, baking soda and water. With an adult's help, place the saucepan on the stove, and turn the heat to medium. Be very careful! Have the adult help you stir the mix constantly. It will start to bubble and get a bit solid. Just keep stirring!

In about 3 minutes, a ball will form. With the adult's help, take the saucepan off the burner to cool. Make sure you turn off that burner! Have the adult spread the ball onto some parchment paper. (Be careful! It will be HOT!) When it is completely cool, you can knead in the baby oil and, if you like, a drop or two of food coloring to give it an extra touch of amazingness. You are now ready to play!

TIPS

Knead in a ½ teaspoon of scented shower gel or a drop or two of your favorite-smelling essential oil to make it uniquely yours.

☐ Store in plastic wrap in an airtight container.

◊ Refresh with water.

CLEAR PLAYDOUGH

ADULT SUPERVISION

DO NOT EAT

This clear playdough is completely insane. You can mold it and shape it like real playdough, but it's clear. It's basically invisible!

INGREDIENTS

1 tsp borax

3 cups (720 ml) water, divided

1 medium-size tube clear peel-off face mask

10 tapioca balls

EQUIPMENT

Mixing bowl

Spoon

Microwave-safe bowl

WHAT YOU DO

In a mixing bowl, mix the borax with 1 cup (240 ml) of water. Squirt the tube of face mask into the bowl and stir together until the dough starts to form. Pull the dough out of the borax-water mixture, add another cup (240 ml) of water to the mixture and roll the dough around in it again until the dough is moldable.

Put the tapioca balls and remaining 1 cup (240 ml) of water into a microwave-safe bowl. With an adult's help, microwave it on high for about 30 seconds, until the water is cloudy. Now, dunk your dough into the tapioca water to give it a matte finish.

TIP

If you want your dough to have a shiny finish instead of a matte one, just skip the tapioca balls!

ADULT SUPERVISION

DO NOT EAT

GLITTER PLAYDOUGH

This glitter dough has extra sparkle for those of you who need a little shine in your lives. For crazy fun, play with it outside and watch the sparkles dance on the table!

INGREDIENTS

3 baby diapers

1 cup (240 ml) water

5 tbsp (120 g) glitter

3 to 5 drops food coloring

2 to 3 tbsp (30 to 45 g) cornstarch

EQUIPMENT

Bowl

WHAT YOU DO

Open up the baby diapers and pour the little balls that are inside into a bowl. Pour the water in to hydrate the balls, and you will have a sticky crystal-like substance. Now, add the glitter, food coloring and cornstarch, and mix with your hands. You'll have a cool, gooey dough!

TIP

Depending on the size of diaper you use, you may need more or less water!

TEXTURED DOUGH

DO NOT EAT

Embrace the mess with this crazy, textured dough. It is full of lumpy, bumpy amazingness! Feel the different textures. Can you tell what they are with your eyes closed?

INGREDIENTS

4 cups (500 g) flour

1½ cups (410 g) salt

3 tbsp (30 g) cream of tartar

2 tbsp (30 ml) liquid coconut oil

2 to 3 cups (480 to 720 ml) cold water

3 drops of your favorite food coloring

½ cup (181 g) play sand (you can find this at a craft or hardware store)

¼ cup (50 g) dry rice

¼ cup (53 g) dry lentils

¼ cup (100 g) aquarium rocks (you can find these at the dollar store)

EQUIPMENT

Plastic bin (11 × 8 × 5 in [28 × 20 × 13 cm] works great)

WHAT YOU DO

Dump the flour, salt, cream of tartar, coconut oil and water in the plastic bin and mix together with your hands until a dough ball forms. Use your fist to punch a hole in the middle of the dough. Place the food coloring, play sand, rice, lentils and aquarium rocks in the hole you made. Knead and squish the dough together.

Try substituting different textured items like dry kidney beans, macaroni noodles or beads. Let your imagination run wild!

☐ Store in an airtight container.

NO-COOK TWO-INGREDIENT DOUGH

DO NOT EAT

Even just making this awesome two-ingredient dough is bound to bring giggles and smiles. It is messy fun.

INGREDIENTS

1 cup (125 g) all-purpose flour

2 to 3 pumps of your favorite liquid hand soap or shower gel

EQUIPMENT

Large bowl

WHAT YOU DO

Dump the flour into a large bowl. Add the hand soap or shower gel. Mix and knead the mixture with your hands. If the mixture is too dry, add another pump of soap or gel. If it is too wet, add more flour. Get your hands good and messy with this one. Mix and knead until it is the consistency you want. Have fun!

TIP

☐ **Store in an airtight container.**

DO NOT
EAT

SHAVING CREAM DOUGH

This dough is super fun to make outside on a warm summer day when you can get good and messy. Make sure you ask an adult before you raid the shaving cream stash to make this awesome light and fluffy dough. It's so fun, it almost bounces!

INGREDIENTS

1 (11-oz [311-g]) can shaving cream

1 cup (160 g) cornstarch

Food coloring (optional)

EQUIPMENT

Large bowl or plastic tub

WHAT YOU DO

Dump the shaving cream into a large bowl or plastic tub. Add the cornstarch into the shaving cream ½ cup (80 g) at a time. Mix and squish it up each time you add the cornstarch. If you like, add a few drops of food coloring to get a cool color effect. Mix and knead the ingredients with your hands until the dough forms a squishy ball. If it is too crumbly, add a little more shaving cream. If it is too wet, add a little more cornstarch.

TIPS

Try different scented shaving creams.

Use cookie cutters to make fun and crazy shapes with the dough.

GLOW-IN-THE-DARK DOUGH

ADULT SUPERVISION

DO NOT EAT

This recipe uses The Best Homemade Playdough (page 78) as a base for this groovy, glowing mixture.

INGREDIENTS

1 batch of The Best Homemade Playdough (page 78)

Glow-in-the-dark paint

WHAT YOU DO

Leave the food coloring out of this batch of The Best Homemade Playdough. Once the dough is cooled and you have formed a ball, take your hands and smash that ball flat. Add about 1 teaspoon at a time of glow-in-the-dark paint. Knead the paint into the dough with your hands. Keep adding paint until it is the color and consistency you want.

If the mixture gets too runny, just add some flour. Hold the completed dough under a bright light for a few minutes. Now you're ready to turn out the lights and have some glowy, doughy fun.

TIPS

For even more vibrant fun, play under a black light!

To recharge the glow, just hold the dough up to a bright light for a few minutes. The glow will be restored, and the fun will continue.

☐ **Store in an airtight container.**

PEANUT BUTTER PLAYDOUGH

EDIBLE

You had me at peanut butter. This dough is as tasty as it is fun! Cut it, smoosh it, roll it, squish it and then eat it! This dough is twice the fun!

INGREDIENTS

1 (16-oz [454-g]) container creamy peanut butter

2 cups (260 g) powdered sugar

EQUIPMENT

Large bowl

WHAT YOU DO

Combine the peanut butter and powdered sugar in a large bowl. Mix it and knead it with your hands until it forms a ball of peanut buttery goodness. Enjoy!

TIPS

Roll the ball in granulated sugar for a touch of texture.

Try crunchy peanut butter for even more texture.

Use 1½ cups (399 g) of peanut butter and ½ cup (133 g) of chocolate hazelnut spread for extra fun yumminess.

☐ **Store in an airtight container.**

🕐 **Limited shelf life.**

JELL-O® DOUGH

What is better than playing with colorful dough? Playing with yummy-smelling colorful dough! You might even be tempted to taste this incredible, edible playtime dough. Watch out, though! Things don't always taste exactly like they smell.

INGREDIENTS

2 cups (250 g) flour

½ cup (137 g) salt

2 tbsp (20 g) cream of tartar

2 tbsp (30 ml) liquid coconut oil

1 (3-oz [85-g]) flavored gelatin packet

1 cup (240 ml) very hot water

EQUIPMENT

2 bowls

Spoon

WHAT YOU DO

Put the flour, salt, cream of tartar and coconut oil into a large bowl. Mix it all together. With an adult's help, place the flavored gelatin into another bowl with the very hot water. Stir it with a spoon until the gelatin is all dissolved.

Now, have the adult pour the hot mixture into your bowl of mixed-up ingredients. Using the spoon, stir all the ingredients together to make a dough. Once the dough cools down, take it out of the bowl, and use your hands to knead it a little on a flat surface. If it is too dry, you can add a little more water. If it is too wet, you can add a little more flour. Time to have some smelly-good fun!

TIPS

Cream of tartar helps dough last a bit longer, but not forever!

☐ **Store in an airtight container.**

🕐 **Limited shelf life.**

CANDY PLAYDOUGH

Everybody loves candy! Mix it with a playdough, and you have instant rainbows of squishy, smooshy fun. Grab a friend, and you'll both be seeing rainbows of awesomeness.

INGREDIENTS

10 to 20 jelly beans in a color of your choice

1 cup (240 ml) water

2 cups (250 g) flour

¼ cup (68 g) salt

2 tbsp (20 g) cream of tartar

1 tbsp (15 ml) liquid coconut oil

EQUIPMENT

Microwave-safe container

Large bowl

Spoon

WHAT YOU DO

Put the jelly beans into a microwave-safe container. Cover them with water and, with an adult's help, heat them in the microwave for 30 seconds. They will be hot.

When the time is up, remove the jelly beans from the water and place the colored water, flour, salt, cream of tartar and coconut oil into a large bowl. Mix it all up. Have an adult help you mix all the ingredients with a spoon until a dough ball forms. Put a good amount of flour on your hands, and clap them above the dough to lightly cover it. This will keep it from being too sticky. Once it is cooled completely, you're ready to play! Repeat with as many colors as you like!

COOKIE DOUGH DOUGH

EDIBLE

Have you ever made cookies at home? They smell tasty, are yummy to nibble and start with a dough much like this one! This fun, good-smelling recipe lets you shape, mold, pretend and, best of all, nibble while you play!

INGREDIENTS

1 cup (80 g) quick-cooking oats

½ cup (63 g) flour

1½ tbsp (15 g) cream of tartar

1½ tbsp (15 g) dry hot chocolate mix

1½ tsp (6 g) brown sugar

1 tsp vanilla extract

2 tbsp (28 g) softened butter or margarine

1 cup (240 ml) cold water

EQUIPMENT

Large bowl

WHAT YOU DO

Mix the oats, flour, cream of tartar, hot chocolate mix and brown sugar in a large bowl. Get in there with your hands! Add the vanilla, butter and cold water. Keep squishing it around. Make sure you squish it between your fingers to mix it up well. Once it's all mixed, you're ready to play!

TIPS

Use chocolate candies, raisins or sprinkles for texture.

Try adding ½ teaspoon of cinnamon to give the dough a yummy pop of flavor.

☐ Store in an airtight container.

🕐 Limited shelf life.

ADULT SUPERVISION

HOMEMADE BUTTER DOUGH

Butter is a fun thing to make at home. You get to use your arm muscles, and a bit of your patience muscle. Once you make your own butter, you can add it to this easy dough recipe for amazing playtime fun.

INGREDIENTS

1½ cups (360 ml) heavy whipping cream

½ cup (137 g) salt, divided

2 cups (250 g) all-purpose flour

2 tbsp (10 g) cream of tartar

¾ cup (180 ml) hot water

EQUIPMENT

Stand mixer or hand mixer

Large bowl

Spoon

WHAT YOU DO

Pour the heavy whipping cream and ¼ teaspoon of the salt into the stand mixer (or a large bowl) and mix until it becomes solid. You made butter!

Now, slowly add the flour, the rest of the salt, the cream of tartar and the hot water to the bowl. Stir it up with the mixer. Once it starts to form a dough, remove it from the bowl and knead it with your hands. You just made your own Homemade Butter Dough!

TIP

Instead of using a mixer, place the heavy whipping cream into a sealed container and shake until solid. This usually takes 8 to 10 minutes.

GALAXY DOUGH

ADULT
SUPERVISION

DO NOT
EAT

Go outside at night, and look up at the sky. Do you see bright stars among the blackness with splashes of blue and purple? This shimmery dough gives you a bit of that galaxy in the palm of your hand.

INGREDIENTS

2 cups (250 g) flour

½ cup (137 g) salt

2 tbsp (20 g) cream of tartar

2 tbsp (24 g) dry strawberry milk powder

1 packet grape powdered drink mix

1 activated charcoal capsule, opened-up to get the powder

2 cups (480 ml) water

1½ tbsp (23 ml) liquid coconut oil

¼ cup (96 g) glitter in your favorite color (we like purple or silver with this dough!)

EQUIPMENT

Large bowl

Saucepan

Spoon

WHAT YOU DO

First things first: get an adult. In a large bowl, mix the flour, salt, cream of tartar, milk powder, drink mix and charcoal. Add the water and coconut oil to a saucepan. With an adult's help, put the saucepan on the stove. Turn the burner to medium heat. Stirring continuously, cook the liquids for about a minute. Then add the dry ingredients to the saucepan. Stir, stir, stir. Keep stirring until a dough forms.

With the adult's help, take the saucepan off the burner, and turn off the burner. Keep stirring the dough. Once it is completely cool, drop it onto a flat surface. Sprinkle in your glitter, and mush it all together. Now you have your own galaxy in your hand!

Add beads or marbles for texture, and to make the galaxy effect even more vibrant.

☐ Store in an airtight container.

🕐 Limited shelf life.

COCONUT PLAYDOUGH

This dough just screams summertime! It will smell like you are playing under a palm tree on a tropical island. Watch out for falling coconuts!

INGREDIENTS

2 cups (250 g) flour

½ cup (137 g) salt

2 tbsp (20 g) cream of tartar

2 tbsp (30 ml) liquid coconut oil

Yellow food coloring

1½ cups (180 ml) very hot coconut water

½ tsp coconut or pineapple extract (optional)

EQUIPMENT

Large bowl

Spoon

Microwave-safe container

WHAT YOU DO

In a bowl, mix together the flour, salt, cream of tartar, coconut oil and food coloring. With an adult's help, heat up the coconut water in the microwave for 90 seconds and carefully add it to the mixture. Stir it all up, using the spoon, until a dough forms. Once it is cool enough, you can turn the mixture out onto a play surface.

To add the optional extract, form the dough into a ball. Use your fist to smash a hole in the middle. Add the extract to the hole. Squeeze, smoosh and mush the dough until it's all mixed up. Now enjoy your yummy-smelling tropical dough.

You can substitute regular water for the coconut water if you don't have it, the dough just won't smell as tropical.

☐ **Store in an airtight container.**

🕐 **Limited shelf life.**

ROCK SALT DOUGH

ADULT SUPERVISION

DO NOT EAT

You've seen rock salt. People use it to whir up homemade ice cream. It can also be used to melt icy roads in the winter. Now you can use it to make an awesome fun dough!

INGREDIENTS

2½ cups (313 g) flour

1¼ cup (341 g) rock salt (ice cream salt), divided

3 tbsp (45 ml) vegetable oil

1 packet of your favorite powdered drink mix (colored is optional)

¾ cup (180 ml) very hot water

EQUIPMENT

Large bowl

Spoon

WHAT YOU DO

Mix the flour, 1 cup (273 g) of the rock salt, the vegetable oil and the drink mix in a large bowl. Have an adult help you add the very hot water to the bowl. Mix it up with a spoon until it forms a dough.

When it is cool to touch, turn it onto your play surface. Work it with your hands until you get a squishy ball. If it is too dry, add more water. If it is too wet, add more flour. Roll the completed dough in the rest of the rock salt. You will end up with a textured glob of fun to shape, mold, create and imagine.

Replace some of the powdered drink mix with pink Himalayan salt crystals for a slight pop of color.

☐ **Store in an airtight container.**

🕒 **Limited shelf life.**

KOOL-AID®
PLAYDOUGH

Grape, cherry, orange, maybe lime? What is your favorite Kool-Aid® flavor? Now you can make your favorite flavors into a fabulous and fun playtime dough. It smells scrumptious, and is a blast to play with!

INGREDIENTS

1 cup (125 g) flour, plus a small handful

1¼ cups (68 g) salt

1 tsp cream of tartar

1 tbsp (15 ml) vegetable oil

2 Kool-Aid® packets

¾ cup (180 ml) water

EQUIPMENT

Microwave-safe bowl

Heat-resistant spatula

WHAT YOU DO

Dump the flour, salt, cream of tartar, vegetable oil, Kool-Aid® packets and water into a bowl. Mix it all up until it's good and combined. With an adult's help, place the bowl into the microwave and heat it for 60 seconds. Be careful! It will be very hot! Have the adult stir up the mixture, making sure to scrape down the sides of the bowl. Let it sit for a minute to set. Add a small handful of flour to your play surface. Dump the dough onto it, and knead it until it is good and elastic. Smell the fruity goodness!

TIPS

You might want a little flour on your hands when you knead the dough at the end. This will keep the dough from sticking to your hands.

☐ Store in an airtight container.

🕐 Limited shelf life.

COLOR-SURPRISE DOUGH

ADULT SUPERVISION

DO NOT EAT

This dough is fun to make for parties. The dry ingredients are mixed and put into baggies ahead of time. When you are ready to play, add the wet ingredients, and surprise! Magical colored-dough time!

INGREDIENTS

FOR EACH BAGGIE

Dry watercolor paints

1 cup (125 g) flour, divided in half

¼ cup (68 g) salt

2 tbsp (20 g) cream of tartar

FOR LATER

4 tsp (20 ml) vegetable oil, divided

1⅓ cups (320 ml) hot water, divided into ⅓ cup (80 ml) portions

EQUIPMENT

Bowl

4 resealable sandwich bags

4 cups or mugs

WHAT YOU DO

First, take your dry watercolor paints, crush them up individually and separate them by color. Mix together ½ cup (63 g) of flour with the salt and cream of tartar in a bowl. Open the sandwich bags, placing each bag in a cup or mug to keep it open. Carefully dump ½ cup (63 g) of the dry mixture in each bag. Add about half of one of your crushed dry watercolor paints to the middle, being careful not to mix it in. Top with ½ cup (63 g) of reserved flour. Seal the bag, carefully squeezing the air out of the bag.

WHEN READY TO USE

Have an adult help you. Add 1 teaspoon of oil to each bag. Squish it around with your hands. Have an adult add ⅓ cup (80 ml) of hot water to each bag, and squish it around. By this time, you should see your dough color! When it is cool enough, dump it on a play surface. Knead, squish and squash it together with your hands. Add more flour if it's too wet. Add more water if it's too dry. Have fun!

TIP

These can be made ahead for "Mom, I'm bored" moments.

WASHABLE SOAP PLAY-DOUGH

ADULT SUPERVISION

DO NOT EAT

Want to make that adult in your life smile? Try this Washable Soap Playdough. You get all the ooey gooey fun, but it's going to keep your hands super easy to wash when it's time to clean up.

INGREDIENTS

3½ cups (438 g) flour

1½ cups (410 g) salt

2 tbsp (20 g) cream of tartar

2 tbsp (30 ml) olive oil

2 cups (480 ml) water

1 cup (240 ml) of your favorite-smelling hand soap or shower gel

5 drops each of 4 or 5 different food colorings

EQUIPMENT

Bowl

Large saucepan

Spoon

WHAT YOU DO

Mix the flour, salt and cream of tartar in a bowl. With an adult's help, place a saucepan on the stove on medium-low heat. Combine the oil, water and soap or shower gel in the saucepan. Stir it up. Heat until it steams, but not until it boils. Take the saucepan off the burner and turn the burner off. Add your dry ingredients to the saucepan. Mix it all up with a spoon. It will be sticky, but keep stirring.

Once it has cooled down, transfer the dough from the saucepan to a clean surface. Knead and squish it with your hands until it is your desired consistency. Squish it into about 4 or 5 pieces. Roll the pieces into balls. Make a dimple in the top of each of your dough balls using your fist. For each dimple, drop in about 5 drops of a food coloring. Knead each ball until the color is all mixed in. Now you can play with one color of dough alone, or you can mix them to create a rainbow of colors!

TIPS

If the dough is too sticky, add more flour. If it is too thick, add more soap or shower gel.

☐ **Store in an airtight container.**

DINO-DIG PLAYDOUGH

Greetings, junior paleontologists. Welcome to a hands-on adventure with "buried fossils." This dough is so easy and fun to make, and it will keep you busy for a Jurassic period (maybe not quite that long)!

INGREDIENTS

2 cups (480 ml) water

1½ cups (187 g) flour

1 packet hot chocolate mix

1 cup (273 g) salt

2 tbsp (30 ml) vegetable oil

⅓ cup (37 g) ground flax seed

⅓ cup (28 g) coffee grounds

Plastic dinosaur toys or bones

EQUIPMENT

Saucepan

Spoon

Wax paper

Craft stick

WHAT YOU DO

Over low heat in a saucepan, mix the water, flour, hot chocolate mix, salt and oil together and stir until the dough is formed. Let your dough cool and pull it out of the pan onto wax paper. Knead the dough together until it is fully mixed. Add in your ground flax seed and coffee grounds. This helps give it that "dirt" look! Then add in your dinosaur toys or bones. Bury them in and then "excavate" them using your hands or a craft stick. Have fun burying your dinosaur bones and excavating them over and over again like a real paleontologist!

TIPS

If your dough is too oily, just add in some extra flour.

☐ Store in an airtight container.

⬦ Refresh with water.

OTHER MOLDABLES

It's not exactly a smooth dough, and it's not exactly a glossy slime. Mix science with play, and an occasional touch of sparkle, and you get these crazy concoctions of awesomeness. Who knew such simple ingredients could come together to make such an incredible playtime delight?

Use dish soap to make Silly Putty (page 139) or you can even go to the moon (page 129). It doesn't matter if you're letting Kinetic Sand (page 125) slip slowly through your hands or using clay to make air-dry pots (page 164), this chapter is nothing but fun!

KINETIC SAND

DO NOT EAT

Think of sitting at the beach and making sand castles. Sand is so fun. Make it a dough, and your sand turns into over-the-top amazingness! This sand makes the best sand castles and anything else your imagination can squish together.

INGREDIENTS

2 cups (724 g) fine play sand (you can find this at a craft or hardware store)

1 tbsp (10 g) cornstarch

2 tsp (10 ml) dish soap

½ tsp coconut oil

3 drops of your favorite food coloring

¼ cup (60 ml) water (you will probably not use it all)

EQUIPMENT

Large bowl

WHAT YOU DO

Dump the sand into the bowl. Add the cornstarch, dish soap, coconut oil and the food coloring if you desire. Squish it around with your hands. Add just enough water so it is not too hard. It should be firm, but moldable. Congratulations! You just made your very own kinetic sand!

CRUNCHY CLOUD DOUGH

DO NOT EAT

We've all spent a lazy day staring up at the clouds, finding different shapes and thinking about what it would be like to actually touch them. Well, now you can! So stop daydreaming, and let's make some superfun, supermoldable Crunchy Cloud Dough!

INGREDIENTS

4 cups (500 g) all-purpose flour

½ cup (120 ml) vegetable oil

1 tbsp (15 g) powdered food coloring (or food coloring that is oil-based)

2 cups (96 g) mini Styrofoam balls (also known as faux snow)

EQUIPMENT

Large bowl

Plastic cup

Spoon or craft stick

Large tub

Toys and cookie cutters (optional)

WHAT YOU DO

Pour the all-purpose flour into the large bowl and set aside. Mix the vegetable oil and food coloring together in the plastic cup, making sure the powder totally dissolves into the oil. Slowly pour the colored oil mixture into the all-purpose flour and mix it all together until the flour is colored evenly. Now, pour the Styrofoam balls into the bowl and use your hands to mix it all together. Move your dough over to a big tub and throw some cookie cutters and toys in the mix for all sorts of fun!

TIPS

If you want your Crunchy Cloud Dough to be extra vibrant, double or even triple the food coloring!

☐ Store in an airtight container.

DO NOT
EAT

MOON DOUGH

Create supersoft mounds of billowy fluff. This dough is like no other. Watch out. This dough is supermessy, but it is a breeze to clean up!

INGREDIENTS

4 cups (500 g) flour or baby powder

½ cup (120 ml) baby oil

2 tbsp (30 ml) baby lotion

EQUIPMENT

Plastic craft bin

WHAT YOU DO

Pour the flour or baby powder into the plastic craft bin. Drizzle the baby oil on top of the flour. Add the baby lotion. Squish and squeeze it together with your hands. It will be soft and moldable. That's it!

TIPS

This is a messy craft! You want to do this one outside, or over a flooring other than carpet. It is easy to clean up, but carpet likes to eat it.

☐ **Store in an airtight container.**

COLD PORCELAIN CLAY

ADULT SUPERVISION

DO NOT EAT

This clay has been used by artists to make sculptures. You can do the same. Whip up a batch of this clay and build your masterpiece.

INGREDIENTS

1 cup (160 g) cornstarch

1 (4-oz [118-ml]) bottle white school glue

2 tbsp (30 ml) lemon juice

2 tbsp (30 ml) baby oil

Handful of flour

Hand lotion (just enough to coat your hands)

Acrylic paints

EQUIPMENT

Microwave-safe bowl

Spoon

Plastic wrap

Airtight plastic container

WHAT YOU DO

Mix the cornstarch, glue, lemon juice and baby oil slowly in the bowl until they are combined into a paste-like substance. Stir for about 4 or 5 more minutes. You want to make sure you get all the clumps out and it is a smooth liquid. Have an adult help you put the mixture into the microwave. Here is the important part: you are going to microwave it in 15-second intervals, and stir it vigorously for 1 minute in between intervals. It will get thicker and thicker. You want to repeat this step until you get a sticky dough that can be formed into a ball with your spoon. You will still have a good amount sticking to the sides of the bowl. This may take 6 to 9 turns in the microwave.

Now, take a handful of flour and shake it over a clean, flat work surface. Rub the lotion on your hands to coat them. When it's cool, take out the sticky blob from the bowl. Place it on your work surface, scraping the sides of the bowl to get all the goo out. Knead this slimy goo until it becomes a dough that is no longer sticky (about 10 minutes).

Here is the waiting part. Wrap it tightly in plastic wrap, and place it in your airtight container. Let it sit for a good 24 hours. When the time is up, you can sculpt this moldable clay. Let your creation air dry until it's completely hard. Once it's dry, you can paint it with acrylic paints.

FROZEN TUNDRA

ADULT SUPERVISION

DO NOT EAT

Year-round snow? This is just what is needed on a hot summer day or in celebration of a snow day. Frozen Tundra is a cold dough, perfect for making snowballs, snowmen or just chilling.

INGREDIENTS

½ cup (120 ml) unscented lotion

⅔ to 1 cup (43 to 125 g) corn flour (also known as masa)

1 tsp white minty toothpaste

1½ tbsp (26 g) grated white sidewalk chalk (optional)

EQUIPMENT

Bowl

Spoon

Cheese grater (optional)

Plastic wrap

WHAT YOU DO

In a bowl, mix together the lotion and corn flour with the spoon. Stir in the toothpaste to give your mixture a kick of mint. If desired, with the help of an adult, grate in the white sidewalk chalk for a snowy color. Mix it well. The mixture should be a doughy consistency that forms easily into a ball shape. Tightly cover the dough ball in plastic wrap. Place it in the freezer. Take the ball out of the freezer after 45 minutes. Uncover it, and throw the plastic wrap away. There you have it! Cold snow.

TIPS

Play until the "snow" isn't cold anymore. You can always place it back in the freezer to recharge the cold.

Substitute colored sidewalk chalk to make your tundra more vibrant.

FAKE SNOW

DO NOT EAT

Snow is cold, melts and appears only during certain times of the year. Not with this fake snow! It's uberfun, and you can make it anytime you want. Don't worry if it gets a bit messy. This snow is easy to sweep or vacuum right up!

INGREDIENTS

1 (8-oz [227-g]) box baking soda

1½ cups (180 g) shaving cream (doesn't have to be exact— eyeball it)

2 drops of your favorite essential oil (optional)

EQUIPMENT

Plastic tablecloth

Plastic craft tub

WHAT YOU DO

Cover your work area with a plastic tablecloth. Dump the entire box of baking soda into the craft tub. Squirt in your shaving cream. Mix all that up with your hands for about 30 seconds. Now you can add 2 drops of essential oil if you desire. Keep mixing with those hands. The "snow" will form pretty quickly. Shape it and mold it as desired.

TIP

This is the perfect time to make a miniature "snow" man.

OVEN CLAY

Do you fancy yourself an artist? This classic clay recipe has been used by many artists. It's easy to make and dries in the oven rather quickly.

INGREDIENTS

2 cups (250 g) flour

1 cup (273 g) salt

2 tbsp (30 ml) coconut oil

½ to 1 cup (120 to 240 ml) water

Acrylic paints

EQUIPMENT

Bowl

Spoon

Baking sheet

Paint brush

WHAT YOU DO

Add the flour, salt and coconut oil to a bowl and mix well. Add the water a little at a time, stirring until you get a clay consistency (you may not use all the water). Take the clay out and make whatever shape your heart desires.

Preheat the oven to 250°F (121°C). Place your clay shapes on a baking sheet, and have an adult place the sheet in the preheated oven. Bake for 30 minutes to 1 hour. Keep an eye on your creations. You want them to get hard, but not burn (until the edges are slightly brown). The size and thickness of your creations will determine how long they need to bake. If you make them too thick, they will crack.

When they are hard, have an adult take them out of the oven. Let them cool completely. Once they are done, you can paint them with acrylic paints to finish them off.

EMOTIONAL STRESS-RELIEVING SACK

ADULT SUPERVISION

DO NOT EAT

Like the Stress Ball recipe (page 138), this one is easier to make with two people. It feels totally cool, and keeps its squished shape when you squeeze it. You have to check it out!

INGREDIENTS

2 (12-in [30-cm]) party balloons

¼ to ½ cup (48 to 96 g) The Best Homemade Playdough (page 78)

EQUIPMENT

Permanent marker (optional)

Scissors

WHAT YOU DO

Cut the neck off of one of the balloons. Have a friend open up this balloon as wide as they can. Fill this balloon with some of The Best Homemade Playdough. Have your friend open up the second balloon as wide as they can. Fit it over the first balloon, open end first. Tie off the second balloon so it is secure. If you desire, draw your current emotion (happy, sad, angry or excited) on the sealed balloon. Squeeze and watch the stress fade away!

TIP

Glue on feathers for hair, googly eyes or buttons for a superspecial squeeze ball.

STRESS BALL

DO NOT EAT

First of all, this is a two-person job, so grab a friend. Double the recipe, and make one for each of you! You both can be squeezing your way to bliss in mere minutes.

INGREDIENTS

3 colorful balloons

½ cup (125 g) flour or ½ cup (181 g) play sand

1 empty water or soda bottle

1 (4-oz [118-ml] or 5-oz [147-ml]) bottle white or clear school glue

EQUIPMENT

Funnel

Popsicle stick (or you can use a dull pencil)

Scissors

WHAT YOU DO

Lay your balloons out in front of you. Blow one of the balloons up two or three times, but then let the air out each time. This will stretch out the balloon and make it easier to fill.

Next, get your funnel. Use it to pour the flour or play sand into the empty bottle. Attach the neck of the stretched-out balloon onto the opening of the bottle. Turn the bottle upside down, and pour the flour or sand into the balloon. You may not have to use all of it. This is okay. Just fill the balloon up to its neck.

Carefully take the balloon off the bottle. Use the popsicle stick to make sure the flour or sand is all packed down into the balloon. The more full it is, the stiffer a stress ball you will have. Carefully cut the neck off the balloon. Then cut the neck off the second balloon. Have a friend stretch open the second balloon as wide as they can get it. Fit it over the open end of the balloon filled with flour or sand. Then cut the neck of the third balloon. Have a friend stretch open the third balloon as wide as they can. Put it over the cut end of your balloon ball. Take your glue and run it along the inside opening of the third balloon. Use just a tiny bit of glue. This will keep the balloon from slipping. Now you have a stress ball you can squish around in your hand!

DISH SOAP SILLY PUTTY

DO NOT EAT

What an easy craft to make when you are in need of some slimy, gooey fun! Grab these two ingredients and go for it. You'll whip this up in no time.

INGREDIENTS

¼ cup (60 ml) dish soap

½ cup (80 g) cornstarch

EQUIPMENT

Bowl

Spoon

WHAT YOU DO

Combine the dish soap and cornstarch in a bowl using the spoon. When the mixture starts to pull away from the bowl, use your hands to knead and squish it up. If it's too dry, add more soap. If it's too wet, add more cornstarch. That's it! Now you have Dish Soap Silly Putty.

TIPS

Add a few drops of food coloring to give the putty a zing of color.

Add a few drops of essential oil to make the putty smell scrumptious.

☐ **Store in an airtight container.**

EDIBLE PUTTY

EDIBLE

It's not a meal, but it's certainly fun to nibble on while you play. It's hard to believe that just three ingredients can be so fun, but check it out! You can squeeze and squish this putty, but still manage to sneak a bite while you create.

INGREDIENTS

2 (3-oz [85-g]) packets flavored gelatin

¾ cup (120 g) cornstarch

¼ cup (60 ml) water

EQUIPMENT

Bowl

Spoon

WHAT YOU DO

Add the gelatin and cornstarch to the bowl. Mix this up with a spoon. Add a teaspoon of water at a time, stirring continuously. Add just enough water to make the dough pull away from the sides of the bowl. Now you can play with it using your hands. So simple!

TIPS

☐ **Store in an airtight container.**

🕐 **Limited shelf life.**

FISHNET SQUISH BALL

ADULT SUPERVISION

DO NOT EAT

This is literally amazeballs. It is a squishy ball that changes its bubbly shape when you squeeze it. Then bubbles of rubbery slime poof out between the netting. You can do it!

INGREDIENTS

1 batch of Laundry Soap Slime (page 50)

1 disposable water bottle

1 balloon

1 pair fishnet stockings (you can find this in the hosiery aisle of most stores)

EQUIPMENT

Scissors

Chopstick or dull pencil

WHAT YOU DO

Make your Laundry Soap Slime. With an adult's help, cut the water bottle in half using the scissors. Be careful. It may be sharp on the cut edge. Recycle the bottom of the bottle. Fit the opening of the balloon over the mouthpiece of the bottle so it resembles a funnel. Put about ½ cup (120 ml) of the slime into the open water bottle. Shove the slime into the balloon using the chopstick or pencil. You should fill the balloon up to its neck with slime.

Take the balloon off the water bottle. Tie the balloon closed. Push the balloon all the way down into the foot of the fishnet stocking. It should be snug. Cut the fishnet stocking, leaving room to tie it. Tie the fishnet stocking to close it. Now, squish your Fishnet Squish Ball. Watch it bubble out between the holes of the fishnet stocking. Pretty cool, huh?!

YOGURT PUTTY

Yogurt and putty. Definitely two words you don't often see together. Pick your favorite flavor of yogurt and spend some quality time playing.

INGREDIENTS

1 cup (235 g) smooth yogurt (no fruit chunks)

Food coloring (optional)

2 cups (320 g) cornstarch

EQUIPMENT

Bowl

Spoon

WHAT YOU DO

Dump the yogurt into a bowl. If you want color, add a few drops of food coloring to the yogurt and mix well. Stir in the cornstarch about a tablespoon (10 g) at a time. Stir each time you add cornstarch. You want the mixture to start to pull away from the sides of the bowl when you stir it. Now, get in there with your hands! Knead and stretch this cool mixture until it's not sticky anymore.

TIP

This putty does NOT store. Throw it away when you're done, and make a new batch the next time you want to play.

DO NOT EAT

FOREVER BUBBLES

Everyone loves bubbles. They make people cheer and giggle with glee as they dance and float in the air. They are even better when they are difficult to pop! Adding two ingredients to your bubble solution turns into infinite soapy fun.

INGREDIENTS

1 cup (240 ml) dish soap

1 cup (240 ml) light corn syrup

¼ cup (60 ml) bubble solution

EQUIPMENT

Bowl

Spoon

Bubble wand

WHAT YOU DO

Mix the dish soap, corn syrup and bubble solution in a bowl with a spoon. Use the bubble wand to blow bubbles. That's it!

TIP

Use different water-safe toys to experiment with blowing different bubbles.

KOOL-AID® FOAM

ADULT SUPERVISION

DO NOT EAT

Watch it grow and change its frothy shape as you create this supercool foam. Then bury your hands in it. Try to squeeze it. Make tunnels in it. Play until it loses its foamy shape.

INGREDIENTS

½ cup (120 ml) water

2 tbsp (30 ml) dish soap

2 Kool-Aid® packets

EQUIPMENT

Large bowl

Spoon

Electric mixer (handheld is okay)

Plastic craft tub

WHAT YOU DO

Combine the water, dish soap and Kool-Aid® packets in a large bowl. Stir with a spoon until it's evenly mixed. Get out your mixer and, with an adult's help, start whipping up the mixture on medium speed. The more you whip it, the bigger the foam will get. When you are done, dump the mixture into your craft tub. Have fun!

TIPS

Use plastic, water-safe toys to play in the foam.

When the foam starts to shrink, you can ask an adult to help you regrow the bubbles by using the electric mixer again.

SQUISHY FUZZ BALL

DO NOT EAT

Little fuzzy balls suspended in jelly-like goo. This just sounds superincredible. It's even more wild when you figure out you can hold this glob in your hands. Your friends are about to be jealous!

INGREDIENTS

Water (about ½ cup [120 ml], depending on size of water bottle)

Clear school glue (about ½ cup [120 ml], depending on size of water bottle)

¼ cup (12 g) fuzz balls

Transparent latex balloon

EQUIPMENT

Empty disposable water bottle

WHAT YOU DO

Get your empty water bottle. Fill it about halfway with water and halfway with glue, leaving some room at the top. After the glue has settled, drop in the fuzz balls.

Blow up the transparent balloon about halfway. Twist the neck of it a couple times so the air does not escape, but do not tie it yet. Fit the open end of the balloon on the open mouth of the bottle. Turn the bottle upside down. Dump the contents of the water bottle into the balloon. Carefully separate the balloon and the bottle. Don't let the liquid come out of the balloon! Tie the balloon. Now you have a squirmy, wormy, colorful, clear balloon that you can play with! Don't bounce this ball. It will pop!

TIP

For extra sparkle, add 2 tablespoons (48 g) of your favorite glitter to the water bottle before you transfer the contents into the balloon.

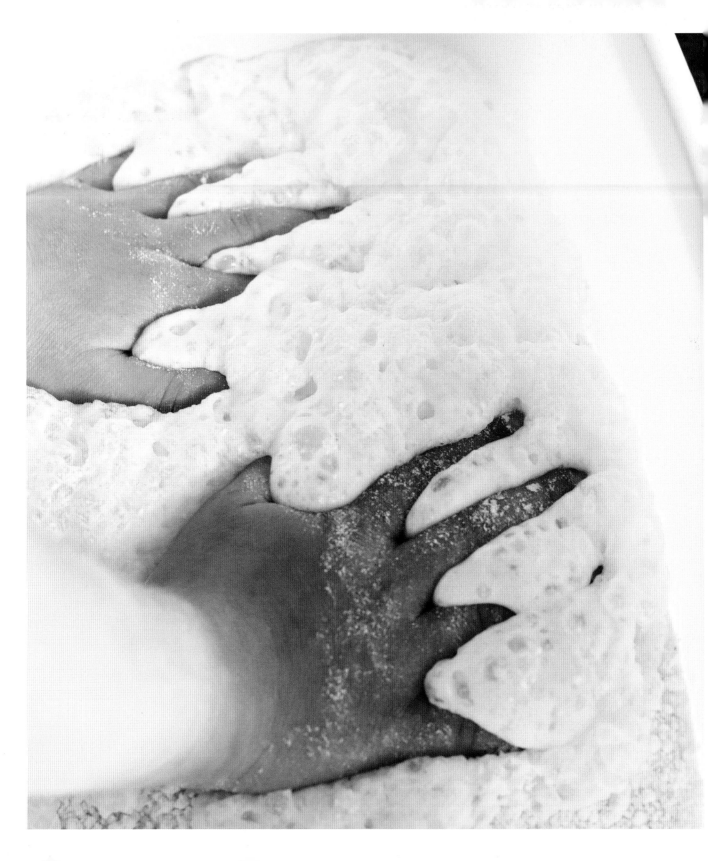

FIZZY DOUGH

It's dough. That erupts. You read that right! First you play with your cool homemade dough, then you transform it into erupting fizz!

INGREDIENTS

1 cup (120 g) flour

1 (8-oz [227-g]) box baking soda

¼ cup (60 ml) liquid coconut oil

¼ cup (60 ml) white vinegar

EQUIPMENT

Plastic craft tub

Spoon

WHAT YOU DO

Mix together the flour, baking soda and coconut oil in your plastic tub, using the spoon. You can play with this like Moon Dough (page 129) until you want to move on to the next step. When you are ready for a change, slowly pour the vinegar over the mixture. Watch it fizz, fizz, fizz. Feel the different texture once the vinegar reacts to the baking soda.

TIP

Try different utensils to pour the vinegar. Try an eye dropper, spoon, baby syringe or whatever your imagination can think of. The more vinegar you drop at one time, the more foam you will create.

OOBLECK

ADULT SUPERVISION

DO NOT EAT

Is it a solid? Is it a liquid? Yes and yes. This is just about the coolest science-experiment-turned-craft ever! Move it, and it's solid. Stop moving it, and it's a liquid.

INGREDIENTS

1 cup (160 g) cornstarch

⅓ cup (80 ml) water

2½ tbsp (38 ml) thick liquid laundry detergent (Tide® works well)

3 drops food coloring

EQUIPMENT

Bowl

Spoon

WHAT YOU DO

Mix the cornstarch, water, laundry detergent and food coloring in the bowl using the spoon. The mixture will get very hard to stir. At this point, get your hands in there. Try to squish the mixture between your fingers. You know it has turned into Oobleck when you can squeeze it into a solid ball shape in your hands, but when you release pressure, the mixture falls like a liquid back into the bowl. This is so cool to make!

DO NOT EAT

LEMON OOBLECK

Why do you think these ingredients together make Oobleck? The acid in the lemons is what helps activate this liquid . . . or solid . . . or liquid gooey substance. You become a scientist with a lemon-smelling lab.

INGREDIENTS

1 cup (160 g) cornstarch

2 good-size lemons

1½ cups (360 ml) water

EQUIPMENT

Bowl

Juicer

Spoon

WHAT YOU DO

Dump the cornstarch into a bowl. Using a juicer, add the juice of the 2 lemons into the bowl, and stir, stir, stir. Add the water a little bit at a time. Stir it up really well with the spoon each time you add water. It is done when you have a solid substance if you try to stir it, but a thick liquid if you leave it alone. How cool is that? You just made Lemon Oobleck using all-natural kitchen ingredients!

TIP

Add 4 drops of yellow food coloring if you want your Oobleck to have a more lemony color.

MAGIC MUD

Let's make potato Magic Mud! Wait. Stop. Does that say potatoes? Yes! Potatoes have supercool properties that can be transformed into magic mud! It is much like Oobleck (page 152), but it's purely made with potatoes and water.

INGREDIENTS

1 (5-lb [2.25-kg]) bag baking potatoes

2 quarts (2 L) hot water (or enough to cover the potatoes)

2 cups (480 ml) room-temperature water

EQUIPMENT

Food processor or food chopper (optional)

2 very large bowls

Strainer

Spoon

Large jar that seals (a large mason jar will work)

WHAT YOU DO

Wash the potatoes under cold water until clean. Dice the cleaned potatoes. Use the food processor or food chopper with an adult's help to make the job easier. Put the diced potatoes into one of the bowls. Add the hot water, just enough to cover the diced potatoes. Stir continuously for 5 minutes. You will notice the water turn reddish-brown. This is normal. Strain the potato water into the second bowl. Let this sit for about 15 minutes. After a few moments you will see a cream-colored mixture at the bottom of the bowl. It will grow larger over the 15 minutes.

Now, pour the water out. Don't worry, the white mixture will stay in the bottom of the bowl. You now need to clean this mixture. Pour the room-temperature water in with the white residue. Mix this with a spoon until it is combined. Pour the mixture into the jar, and seal the jar. Shake the jar for 3 minutes, and then let the jar sit for another 15 minutes. Quickly pour the water out, and you will be left with a clean, white substance. Pour this substance into a bowl. You now have your magic mud. Try to squish it and move it around. It acts much like Oobleck. Do you know why this is? It acts much like Oobleck in that it's both a liquid and a solid gooey mixture!

Use the diced potatoes that are left over to make soup, hash browns, latkes or something yummy.

Add a few drops of food coloring for a pop of color.

BOUNCY BALL

ADULT
SUPERVISION

DO NOT
EAT

Everyone loves a good bouncy ball. But did you ever think you could make one at home? How high can you bounce your own bouncy ball?

INGREDIENTS

1 tbsp (15 ml) white school glue

3 drops food coloring

2 tbsp (30 ml) warm water

½ tsp borax

½ tbsp (10 g) cornstarch

EQUIPMENT

2 disposable bowls

2 popsicle sticks

WHAT YOU DO

Pour the school glue into a disposable bowl. Using a popsicle stick, mix the food coloring into the glue until it is an even color. In the second bowl, mix the water and borax together using the second popsicle stick. Combine the mixture until the borax is completely dissolved. Add the cornstarch and a ½ teaspoon of the borax solution to the glue mixture. Let it stand for 20 seconds.

Now, stir the mixture together with a popsicle stick until it becomes very hard to stir. Take half of the mixture out. Roll it around in your hands until a ball forms. The longer you roll it around in your hands, the more solid it will become. You want it to become as solid as a bouncy ball. When you are done, try to bounce it. Voila! You have your bouncy ball.

TIP

The remaining half of the mixture can be used to make a Fishnet Squish Ball (page 141) or Squishy Fuzz Ball (page 148).

GLOWING MAGIC MUD

As if Magic Mud (page 155) wasn't cool enough, you can make it glow! There are few things as fun as watching, and playing with, a glowy goo. This one is ultracool.

INGREDIENTS

1 batch of Magic Mud (page 155)

2 tbsp (30 ml) tonic water

EQUIPMENT

Bowl

Spoon

Black light

WHAT YOU DO

Get your Magic Mud, and put it in a safe place. Make sure it's uncovered in a bowl. Leave it alone for about 2 days. It will turn into a crumbly, dry, white powder.

Now, take this dry powder and add your tonic water, a little at a time. Stir it up really well with your spoon each time you add the water. It will get really stiff and hard to stir. You will get a workout on your patience here. It might take some time and lots of stirring. Once it resembles the Magic Mud that you made the first time, you are ready. Turn on your black light, and watch the goo glow while you play with it. Look at your hands! They will be glowing too!

You have to use tonic water. Do not substitute a different water.

Why does the goo glow? Tonic water contains quinine. Quinine glows under a black light! Look at the bottle of remaining tonic water. There should be a glowing liquid in the bottle. Supercool!

EDIBLE FAIRY DOUGH

Invoke the powers of the bee with this dough. Break out that honey, and make this glittery work of edible goodness. It wouldn't be fairy dough without the glitter! Make sure to hit it with that special sparkle before you're done.

INGREDIENTS

Cooking spray

¼ cup (60 ml) honey

¾ cup (120 g) cornstarch

1 tbsp (15 ml) liquid coconut oil

4 drops food coloring

2 tbsp (48 g) edible food glitter

EQUIPMENT

¼-cup (60-ml) measuring cup

Bowl

Spoon

WHAT YOU DO

Coat the inside of the measuring cup generously with cooking spray. Fill the measuring cup with honey, and dump it into the bowl. Using the spoon, add about 1 tablespoon (10 g) at a time of the cornstarch to the honey and stir the mixture. Keep adding the cornstarch, completely mixing it in before you add more. You will need to add a bit of coconut oil once in a while to make sure the mixture isn't too sticky. When it gets too hard to incorporate the cornstarch with the spoon, coat your hands with the cooking spray and squish the mix together with your hands.

Add the food coloring and squish together. Add the edible food glitter, and squish together until the dough is completely mixed up. Now you can play with this fairy dough. Stretch it, knead it and roll it into a ball. Don't forget that it is completely edible. If you want to sneak a nibble here and there, go for it!

ADULT SUPERVISION

DO NOT EAT

FLOAM

You have certainly held this substance before. Did you ever think, in your most fantastical dreams, that you'd be able to re-create it at home? Yes, you can!

INGREDIENTS

2½ tsp (23 g) borax

¾ cup (180 ml) hot (not boiling) water, divided

1 (5-oz [147-ml]) bottle clear school glue

½ cup (24 g) foam balls (bean-bag filler)

EQUIPMENT

2 bowls

Spoon

WHAT YOU DO

Ask an adult to help you mix the borax with ⅓ cup (80 ml) of hot water in a bowl until completely dissolved. Combine the remaining hot water and the glue in a second bowl. Slowly stir in the borax water. If the mixture is too wet, add a little more borax. If it is too dry, add more water. Stir continuously while you add the foam balls. When it gets too hard to stir with a spoon, knead it together with your hands. You should now have Floam! What shapes can you create?

TIPS

Add 3 drops of food coloring to the mixture before you add the foam balls. This will give it a pretty hint of color.

☐ Store in an airtight container.

COCONUT OIL SHAKY DOUGH

What a supereasy dough! It makes cleanup a breeze. Just some shakes and rolls of the bag, and it magically appears.

INGREDIENTS

⅓ cup (80 ml) coconut oil

½ small bottle of food coloring (optional)

1½ cups (186 g) flour

EQUIPMENT

Microwave-safe container

1 (1-gal [3.75-L]) resealable plastic bag

WHAT YOU DO

With an adult's help, warm up your coconut oil in the microwave for about 30 seconds to melt it. If you like, add food coloring to the oil. Put your flour in the resealable plastic bag. Pour the oil into the bag and shake and knead the dough until it's mixed. Now you have light, fluffy, awesomely easy dough!

AIR-DRY CLAY

DO NOT EAT

Another fun way to make a hardened sculpture! Let that budding artist inside you out! Let your imagination run wild while squishing and shaping this dough. Top your masterpiece off with a splash of color!

INGREDIENTS

½ cup (80 g) cornstarch, plus 1 handful

½ cup (120 ml) white school glue

1 tbsp (15 ml) baby oil

1 tbsp (15 ml) white vinegar

Acrylic paints

EQUIPMENT

Bowl

Spoon

Paintbrush

WHAT YOU DO

Mix the cornstarch, glue, baby oil and vinegar in a bowl with a spoon. You will have a supersticky dough. Sprinkle a handful of cornstarch down on your flat, clean working surface. Take out your dough mixture and place it over the cornstarch. With a little cornstarch covering your hands to prevent sticking, roll and knead your mixture into the cornstarch on the flat surface. You are done when you have a smooth dough. Now you can make it into fun shapes. Let it air dry for about 48 hours. Then get out your acrylic paints and make it your own masterpiece.

TIP

You can store unused dough in a resealable plastic bag with a teaspoon of baby oil.

DO NOT EAT

SAND CLAY

This clay is great for making memory items. Squish your footprint in the dough, and it will look like you just walked across the sand at the beach. Finish it off with some cool decorations or color!

INGREDIENTS

2½ cups (905 g) play sand (you can find this at a craft or hardware store)

2 cups (250 g) flour

1¾ cups (478 g) salt

1½ cups (360 ml) warm water

EQUIPMENT

Plastic craft tub

Spoon

WHAT YOU DO

Dump the play sand, flour and salt into the craft tub. Mix the water in with the spoon until combined. Now comes the fun part. Get your hands in there. Knead and squish it until a dough forms. Add more sand if it is too wet. Add more water if it is too dry. The dough can be split into 5 balls. Each one can be made into the creation you desire.

When your creations are done, let them air dry, or you can place them on a cookie sheet in a 250°F (121°C) oven for 3 to 5 hours, depending on the thickness of the creations.

TIP

This is a great dough to use for children's hand- and footprints. Just roll each ball to about a ½-inch (1.3-cm) thickness, and have the child place their hand or foot in the dough. Dry as directed.

PLAY PUTTY

ADULT SUPERVISION **DO NOT EAT**

Looking for a superquick putty to play with? You found it! Three items squeezed, rolled and mixed in a bag. It can't get much easier than that.

INGREDIENTS

¾ cup (180 ml) liquid starch

½ cup (120 ml) white school glue

¼ cup (60 ml) tempura paint

EQUIPMENT

1 (1-gal [3.75-L]) resealable plastic bag

WHAT YOU DO

Place the starch, glue and paint into the resealable plastic bag. Seal the bag completely. Knead, mix and roll the bag around until all the ingredients are mixed. Presto! You have a fun play putty that is supereasy to make, and even more fun to play with!

 **TIP**

☐ **Store in an airtight container.**

CLEAN MUD

ADULT SUPERVISION

DO NOT EAT

Let's face it, mud is a mess. Only the coolest of the cool kids can make mud that isn't dirty at all! In fact, it's made with soap. It's squeaky-clean, muddy fun.

INGREDIENTS

1 roll toilet paper

1 bar soap (any kind will do)

1 tbsp (36 g) borax (this is completely optional but will make your mud last longer)

4 drops food coloring (optional)

2 to 3 cups (480 to 720 ml) water

EQUIPMENT

Bowl

Cheese grater

Spoon

WHAT YOU DO

Unroll your toilet paper and break it into little pieces. Put the pieces in your bowl. With an adult's help, grate your soap on a cheese grater into the bowl. Mix together the soap and toilet paper (and the borax and food coloring, if you like) with about 2 cups (480 ml) of water. Add more water until your mud is a fun consistency! Boom. Done!

TIPS

Let the mixture sit overnight to get it extra goopy like mud.

☐ Store in an airtight container.

SOFT MUD

It's like jumping in puddles on a rainy day, but much cleaner. Break out your toy pots and pans! I feel some wicked cool mud pies coming on.

INGREDIENTS

2 cups (384 g) baking soda

½ tsp coconut oil

½ cup (120 ml) water

EQUIPMENT

Bowl

WHAT YOU DO

Mix the baking soda, coconut oil and water together in a bowl until the desired consistency is reached. If it is too wet, add more baking soda. If it is too dry, add more water. Bam! That's it!

This can be messy, but it is very easy to clean up. Water will make it melt away.

☐ **Store in an airtight container.**

🕐 **Limited shelf life.**

CEREAL CLAY

ADULT SUPERVISION   **EDIBLE**

Thick like clay. Edible like candy. You simply cannot go wrong with this recipe. Invite your friends over, and everyone can dig into making this cereal clay. Yum!

INGREDIENTS

¼ cup (58 g) real butter, plus more for coating

1 large (16-oz [453-g]) bag of mini marshmallows

1 regular-size box desired cereal

EQUIPMENT

Large saucepan

Large spoon

Plastic craft bin

WHAT YOU DO

Have an adult help you melt the butter in the large saucepan on medium heat. Carefully dump in the bag of marshmallows, and stir continuously until melted. This will be very sticky. With an adult's help, take the saucepan off the burner and turn off the burner. Rub butter all over the spoon, but not on the handle. Mix your cereal in, about a ½ cup (100 g) at a time. This will get harder and harder to stir. Just use those muscles and keep stirring.

Once all the cereal is added, have an adult help you drop the mixture into the craft bin. Put a small amount of butter all over the palms of your hands. If the cereal mixture is cool enough, you can smoosh and mush it around with your hands. The best part . . . you can eat it!!

TIP

Use colored marshmallows, or add 3 drops of your favorite food coloring!!

DO NOT EAT

PUFFY PAINT

Puffy paint is a mystical substance that adds a dimension to ordinary art. Suddenly you are painting in 3D. The possibilities are endless.

INGREDIENTS

1 cup (120 g) shaving cream

⅓ cup (80 ml) white school glue

A few drops food coloring, each in a different color (red, orange, yellow, green, blue or purple)

EQUIPMENT

Large bowl

Craft stick

2 to 3 small bowls or plastic containers

Paintbrush

Paper

WHAT YOU DO

Mix the shaving cream and glue together in the large bowl using the craft stick. Once combined, separate that mixture into smaller bowls or plastic containers (you can skip this step if you are making it all one color). Add a few drops of food coloring to each container, and stir until combined. Repeat for as many colors as you want to make.

Use the paintbrush to "paint" them on the paper. You want to make sure you use a good amount of the paint so it's nice and puffy. When you're done, let your picture dry completely. It will have a fun squishy texture once it is dry!

TIP Layer your paint to see a really cool effect.

HOMEMADE SMILEY-EMOJI SQUISHY

DO NOT EAT

Squishies. The craze is here to stay! Why spend your hard-earned allowance on a store-bought squishy when they are totally easy to make at home? Once you've mastered this smiley emoji, the sky's the limit! What else can you create?

INGREDIENTS

1 round cosmetic sponge (makeup sponge you can cut in a circle)

Yellow, red, black and white fabric paint or Puffy Paint (page 176)

EQUIPMENT

Plastic table cover

Plastic gloves

Small paintbrush

WHAT YOU DO

Cover your work surface in the plastic table cover. Set everything you need out on this cover. The only paint you want to use is either fabric paint or Puffy Paint. These paints are a bit stretchy when dry, and work better for squishing. Wearing the plastic gloves, drop a big glob of the yellow paint onto the sponge. Work the color all around the sponge using your fingers. Make sure you cover the entire sponge. Let the sponge dry completely. Using the paintbrush and the paint, paint eyes and a smile on the front of the sponge. Let it dry completely. You now have a squishable friend you can take with you. You can also tell everyone that you made it with your own hands!

TIP

You can make any shape your imagination can create using the same technique. What can you come up with?

MAGIC GLITTER BOTTLES

ADULT SUPERVISION

DO NOT EAT

This ultracool goopy mixture lives in its very own bottle. It is like your own little miniature world of magical floating sparkly goo. It is mesmerizing!

INGREDIENTS

½ cup (120 ml) warm-to-hot water (roughly)

1 (6-oz [177-ml]) bottle glitter glue

2½ tbsp (60 g) glitter

Clear glue to top off bottle

Super glue

EQUIPMENT

1 (16- or 20-oz [473- or 591-ml]) clean, empty disposable water bottle

WHAT YOU DO

Remove any labels or sticky goo from the outside of the bottle. Fill about ¾ of the water bottle with the warm-to-hot water, leaving room for your glitter glue and glitter. Add the bottle of glitter glue and the glitter to your bottle. Put the lid on the bottle, and shake it well to mix the ingredients together. Your bottle should be filled most of the way up. Add clear glue to top off the bottle.

Have an adult super glue the lid onto the water bottle, and let it dry. Once the lid is completely dry, you will have a magic glitter bottle. You can shake up the bottle so it is a mixture of swirly, twirly glitter. Wait about 5 minutes, and that glitter will all fall to the bottom of the bottle. You can then shake and swirl your bottle, starting the awesome glitter show once again.

TIP

Try using different colors of glue and glitter. You just might want a bottle in every color of the rainbow!

ACKNOWLEDGMENTS

This book would not have been possible without our amazing husbands, Kevin, Brandon and Greg. Thank you for lending us your hands when ours were covered in slime and goop!

Special thanks go to Amanda Moring, Heather Kirk and Brandy Arnold. Y'all are crazy-amazing and gave this book extra-specialness through words, actions and photos. And never once did you question our sanity. Thank you for that!

And to those slime-covered kids who smiled through "one more picture, please," we really appreciate your patience and willingness to be silly with us: Halle Harrington, Lauren Kirk, Katie Kirk, Rachel Kirk, Emma Arnold, Kira Perez, Mia Perez, Kenneth Lewis, Alora Phillips, Abiageal Harding, Savannah Edwards, Jadyn Burkett, Zoe Testerman, Kayzen Pyper, Tarek Pyper, Logan Williams, Jameson Williams, Alex Conway, Ethan Reed, Sadie MacKay, Cameron MacKay and Carter MacKay...whew!

Thank you, thank you, thank you Kate Testerman. Your kindness and candor were much appreciated. We needed both during this process!

And lastly (but definitely not least), a huge thank you to the Page Street Publishing team for once again putting up with our shenanigans and then printing them into something we can't believe is possible. Marissa Giambelluca, you kept us on track in a sweetly persistent way that was much appreciated. And thanks to Meg Baskis who helped imagine this vision from the very beginning. And Will Kiester, thank you again. You ask the hard questions, work tirelessly as a diplomat and keep the faith in us.

ABOUT THE AUTHORS

JAMIE HARRINGTON is the creator of the blog, Totally the Bomb, co-author of *The 101 Coolest Simple Science Experiments* and author of *The Unofficial Guide to Crafting the World of Harry Potter.* She has always had an appreciation for the way playdough squishes in her hands, but she never, ever, ever mixed the colors together. She is now pro color-mixing and encourages everyone to mix the heck out of them!

BRITTANIE PYPER is the author of *Adorkable Bubble Bath Crafts*, writes SimplisticallyLiving.com and fell in love with playdough when she was a little girl. What started with pretend cooking and baking has turned into a DIY obsession for all things ooey and gooey, which doubles as entertainment for her kids.

HOLLY HOMER is the co-author of *101 Kids Activities that are the Bestest, Funnest Ever!* and *The 101 Coolest Simple Science Experiments*. She runs KidsActivities.com and the Quirky Momma Facebook page. It was love at first smell for her and playdough. Making salt dough was one of her earliest memories and her family's Christmas tree still holds her homemade creations.

INDEX